KU-659-977

Economics Express

Macroeconomics

Dean Garratt

PEARSON

Harlow, England • London • New York • Boston • San Francisco • Toronto • Sydney
Auckland • Singapore • Hong Kong • Tokyo • Seoul • Taipei • New Delhi
Cape Town • São Paulo • Mexico City • Madrid • Amsterdam • Munich • Paris • Milan

PEARSON EDUCATION LIMITED
Edinburgh Gate
Harlow CM20 2JE
United Kingdom
Tel: +44 (0)1279 623623
Web: www.pearson.com/uk

First published 2013 (print)

The Financial Times. With a worldwide network of highly respected journalists, The Financial Times provides global business news, insightful opinion and expert analysis of business, finance and politics. With over 500 journalists reporting from 50 countries worldwide, our in-depth coverage of international news is objectively reported and analysed from an independent, global perspective. To find out more, visit **www.ft.com/pearson-offer**.

ISBN: 978-0-273-77610-9 (print)
      978-0-273-77612-3 (PDF)
      978-0-273-78560-6 (eText)

British Library Cataloguing-in-Publication Data
A catalogue record for the print edition is available from the British Library

Library of Congress Cataloging-in-Publication Data
Garratt, Dean, 1970–
  Economics express : macroeconomics/Dean Garratt. – First Edition.
    pages cm
  Includes index.
  ISBN 978-0-273-77610-9
  1. Macroeconomics.   I. Title.
  HB172.5.G3647 2013
  339–dc23
                            2013019175

10 9 8 7 6 5 4 3 2 1
16 15 14 13

Print edition typeset in 9.5/12.5 pt Scene std by 71
Print edition printed in Great Britain by Henry Ling Ltd., at the Dorset Press, Dorchester, Dorset

Contents

Introduction   vii

Acknowledgements   viii

1   Introduction to macroeconomics   1

2   Aggregate demand and national income   29

3   The *AD–AS* model   57

4   The business cycle   79

5   Banking, money and monetary policy   107

6   Unemployment and inflation   139

7   The open economy   169

And finally, before the assessment . . .   203

Glossary   209

Index   217

Supporting Resources

→ **Understand key concepts quickly**

Printable versions of the **Topic maps** give an overview of the subject and help you plan your revision

Test yourself on key definitions with the online **Flashcards**

→ **Revise effectively**

Check your understanding and practise for exams with the **multiple choice questions**

→ **Make your answers stand out**

Evaluate sample exam answers in the **You be the marker** exercises and understand how and why an examiner awards marks

All this and more can be found at www.pearsoned.co.uk/econexpress

Introduction – Economics Express series

From the series editor, Professor Stuart Wall

Welcome to *Economics Express* – a series of short books to help you to:

- take exams with confidence
- prepare for assessments with ease
- understand quickly
- and revise effectively

There has never been a more exciting time to study economics, given the shock to so many individuals, institutions and countries in 2007/8 when long established economic certainties were suddenly brought into question. The so-called 'credit crunch' overpowered both financial and non-financial organisations. Government bail-outs of banks and businesses became the order of the day in many countries, with massive increases in government expenditures to fund these bail-outs, quickly followed by austerity budgets aimed at restoring national debts and budget deficits to pre-credit crunch levels. Looking forward, there is as much talk about 'triple-dip' recessions as there is about recovery.

As you embark on your economic journey, this series of books will be your companions. They are not intended to be a replacement for the lectures, textbooks, seminars or further reading suggested by your lecturers. Rather, as you come to an exam or an assessment, they will help you to revise and prepare effectively. Whatever form your assessment takes, each book in the series will help you build up the skills and knowledge to maximise your performance.

You can find more detail of the features contained in this book and which will help develop your assessment skills in the 'Guided Tour' on page ix.

Series editor's acknowledgements

I am extremely grateful to Kate Brewin and Gemma Doel at Pearson Education for their key roles in shaping this series. I would also like to thank the many lecturers and students who have so helpfully reviewed the key features of this series and whose responses have encouraged us to believe that many others will also benefit from the approaches we have adopted throughout this series.

Stuart Wall

Guided tour of the book

→ ## Understand key concepts quickly

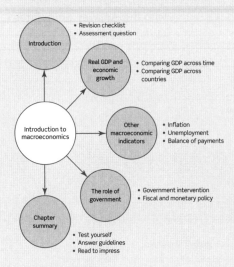

Start to plan your revision using the **Topic maps.**

Grasp **Key definitions** quickly using this handy box. Use the flashcards online to test yourself.

→ ## Revise Effectively

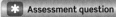

Assessment question

Can you answer this essay-type question? Guidelines on answering the question are presented at the end of this chapter.

With the aid of a diagram, describe the income flows in the circular flow of income model. Using a simple Keynesian model, discuss the impact on national income of a *reduction* in injections into the circular flow.

Prepare for upcoming exams and tests using the **Assessment question** at the start of each chapter.

Answer guidelines

✴ Assessment question

With reference to real-world examples, describe some of the key issues analysed by macroeconomists.

Approaching the question

The question is inviting you to draw out the distinction between micro- and macroeconomic analysis with reference to real-world issues.

Important points to include

- **Distinction between micro- and macroeconomic analysis**. Explain how the focus of the two principal branches of economics differs.
- **Key macroeconomic issues**. Identify the key macroeconomic indicators including: economic growth, inflation, unemployment, the balance of payments and the role that government might be expected to play.
- **Definitions**. In exploring each of the issues, be sure to define carefully and accurately the related concepts, for example real GDP in the case of economic growth.

Compare your responses with the **Answer guidelines** at the end of the chapter.

→ # Make your answers stand out

Check out the additional tips to **Make your answer stand out** at the end of the chapter.

Make your answer stand out

- Try to avoid simply *listing* macroeconomic issues. Show your understanding by drawing on real-world examples, thereby illustrating your awareness of the macroeconomic environment.
- Try to incorporate a range of contemporary examples relating to the four general issues, but if possible drawing on other macroeconomic issues too – for example, issues around government borrowing and the eurozone crisis. Again, the aim is to show your awareness of the macroeconomic environment and current events. Therefore, try to relate to macroeconomic stories that have been in the news.
- Try and draw out historical and international comparisons wherever possible.

Examples & evidence

Consumer Spending and Financial Institutions

Household consumption makes up about two-thirds of aggregate demand in the UK. Understanding its determinants is therefore important in under-standing changes to national income. The obvious starting point is dispos-able income. Over the long term, evidence does indeed show that, after stripping out the effects of rising prices (inflation), disposable income and consumer spending grow at very, very similar rates: about 2½ per cent per annum over the past 50 years or so.

However, the statistical relationship between disposable income and consumption is different in the short term. We can see this in the chart tracking quarter-to-quarter changes in real household spending and real disposable income (%) (opposite). In other words, the chart tracks the real growth in spending and income over three-month periods.

The chart shows that quarterly consumption growth rates are typically less variable than those in disposable income. From this, economists infer that households 'smooth their spending' despite facing volatile incomes. This is known as consumption smoothing.

Consumption smoothing is facilitated by the financial system, enabling us either to borrow to supplement spending or to save to enjoy more spend-ing in the future. Therefore, the financial system can help households to avoid large variations in their spending from, say, month to month. It

Using real-world examples can raise your marks during an exam or assessment. Read the **Examples and evidence** boxes in each chapter.

1 Introduction to macroeconomics

Topic map

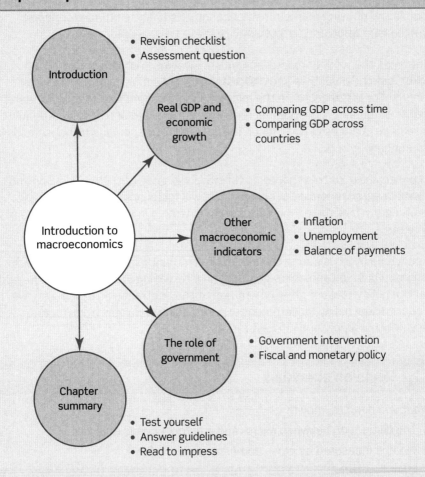

- Revision checklist
- Assessment question

Introduction

Real GDP and economic growth
- Comparing GDP across time
- Comparing GDP across countries

Introduction to macroeconomics

Other macroeconomic indicators
- Inflation
- Unemployment
- Balance of payments

The role of government
- Government intervention
- Fiscal and monetary policy

Chapter summary
- Test yourself
- Answer guidelines
- Read to impress

A printable version of this topic map is available from **www.pearsoned.co.uk/econexpress**

Introduction

Microeconomics is concerned with particular goods, services and resources. It analyses the individual parts of the economy including the interaction between consumers and producers in particular markets. Macroeconomics analyses broader sectors of the economy and, of course, the economy as a whole. Nonetheless, it important to recognise that the objective of both branches of economics is the same: to analyse the implications of our unlimited wants when the resources available to meet these wants are themselves scarce.

Both macroeconomics and microeconomics analyse consumption and production activity. What differs is the level of *focus*. While microeconomists might analyse the behaviour of consumers and suppliers in a particular market, for example the housing market, macroeconomists analyse broader or aggregated consumption and output activity.

Sometimes the work of macroeconomists involves analysing a particular market, but the objective is to understand its potential to affect the wider economy. For instance, while the microeconomist might investigate the determinants of house prices, the macroeconomist might look to investigate how house price changes can influence the total level of spending by households in the economy.

The principal aim of this chapter is to introduce some of the main issues and topics in macroeconomics. In doing so, we will focus on four key issues: the size and growth of the economy, inflation, unemployment and the balance of payments.

We conclude by considering the role of government in affecting these macroeconomic variables and, more generally, in intervening in the economy. We consider the policy tools of government and of the central bank. In doing so, we introduce fiscal policy (government expenditure and taxation) and monetary policy (money supply and interest rates).

 Revision checklist

What you need to know:
- ☐ The distinction between micro- and macroeconomic analysis.
- ☐ What is measured by gross domestic product (GDP).
- ☐ Identify alternatives to GDP as measures of the size of the economy.
- ☐ The distinction between nominal and real GDP.

- ❏ What economists mean by economic growth.
- ❏ What is meant by purchasing-power parity and its significance for comparing GDP across countries.
- ❏ What is meant by the rate of inflation.
- ❏ How we measure unemployment and the rate of unemployment.
- ❏ What is recorded on the balance of payments.
- ❏ Patterns in the UK balance of trade.
- ❏ The macroeconomic policy instruments of government and the central bank.

✱ Assessment question

Can you answer this essay-type question? Guidelines on answering the question are presented at the end of this chapter.

With reference to real-world examples, describe some of the key issues analysed by macroeconomists.

Real GDP and economic growth

As we go through this chapter, we will introduce four key macroeconomic variables. Of these, perhaps the most crucial is the size of the economy. For this reason, we pay particular attention to the size and growth of economies.

The most commonly used measure of economic size is **gross domestic product**, known more simply as GDP. This measures the value of the various goods and services supplied by firms within an economy over a given period, usually a 12-month or 3-month period. The measure focuses on **final goods and services** as opposed to **intermediate goods and services**. Intermediate goods and services are components of final goods and services. An example is sugar purchased by a restaurant as an ingredient for its food and drinks. In this case, the restaurant is not the final user of the sugar, but rather the restaurant's customers are. However, sugar bought by a family in a supermarket for their own consumption is a final good.

GDP does not capture all aspects of economic activity. As we have seen, it relates only to the output of final goods and services. It excludes the exchange of second-hand goods, other than the 'services' which facilitate their exchange, such as the services of exchange agents and car dealers.

It also excludes certain activities, like DIY, gardening and cleaning, when undertaken by individuals themselves. If these activities were purchased, they would be included. GDP estimates are affected when payments for economic activity go unrecorded, for example when goods or services are purchased through underground markets.

Key definitions

Gross domestic product (GDP)
The market value of domestically produced goods and services.

Intermediate goods and services
Goods and services used as inputs that become components of the final good or service.

Final goods and services
Goods and services when purchased by their final or ultimate user rather than as components of a good or service.

GDP measures the output of economic activity *within* a country. However, foreign residents, including foreign-owned firms, earn some of the income generated by economic activity. Therefore, some flows of income go abroad (outflow). Conversely, some of the incomes earned by domestic residents come from abroad (inflow). An alternative measure of economic activity is known as **gross national income** (GNY). This attempts to measure the value of income earned by domestic residents, regardless of the country in which the income is generated. It is calculated as GDP *plus* 'net' income earned abroad (inflows *less* outflows).

Another well-known measure of economic activity is **net national income** (NNY). This takes into account that in the act of production, our physical resources, such as machinery and buildings, are subject to wear and tear and that, primarily because of technological progress, some resources become obsolete. Therefore, our 'gross' measures of economic activity ignore capital depreciation. Net national income is calculated by subtracting from gross national income an allowance for depreciation.

GDP, GNY and NNY provide us with a picture of economic activity, albeit an imperfect one. Equally, they are imperfect measures of national well-being. Measuring national well-being and national 'happiness' is very subjective. We all hold views on the variables that we would want to include in such measures. They could include, for instance, quality of life, environmental damage from economic activity, equality of resources, life expectancy, and so on.

Despite the considerable amount of work on measures of national well-being, GDP remains the principal measure by which economists and non-economists compare economic activity both across time and between countries.

Key definitions

Gross national income

The income earned by domestic residents from economic activity regardless of where that activity occurred. It is estimated by adding net income from abroad to GDP.

Net national income

The income earned by domestic residents after taking into account the depreciation of the nation's physical resources from economic activity.

Recap

The three principal measures of economic activity are gross domestic product (GDP), gross national income (GNY) and net national income (NNY).

Test yourself

Q1. Why do we exclude the purchases of intermediate goods and services in our estimate of GDP?

Q2. How would an increase in the foreign ownership of firms affect GDP?

Comparing GDP across time

An estimate of GDP allows us to say something about the size of the economy at a moment in time. A natural extension of this is to compare the economy's size over time. However, to compare the *volume* of output over time we need to strip out or eliminate the effect that changing prices have on the observed value of GDP.

The observed or actual value of GDP is also known as **nominal GDP**. Nominal GDP captures not only the quantities of goods and services that are produced, but also the prices at which these goods and services are sold. The average price of the economy's output is known as the **GDP deflator**. The GDP deflator tends to increase over time, this will tend to increase the value of nominal GDP even when the output of the economy falls.

In fact, between 1950 and 2011 nominal GDP in the UK fell on only one occasion. This occurred in 2009. However, this does not paint an accurate picture of economic growth. To compare the volume of output, we need to measure GDP with prices held constant. A constant-price measure of GDP is known as **real GDP**. Changes in real GDP reflect only changes in the volume of output.

Key definitions

Nominal GDP

Another name for actual GDP where estimates are affected both by the volume of output and by the prices of the output.

GDP deflator

The name given to the average price level of domestically produced goods and services.

Real GDP

A constant-price estimate of the value of the economy's output measured at the prices of a chosen base year.

✳ Assessment advice

The distinction between nominal and real values is incredibly important in economics. It is therefore essential that you can clearly demonstrate your understanding of this distinction in the context of the size of the economy.

Official estimates of real GDP are constructed using a process known as **chain linking**. The first step involves estimating, for pairs of consecutive years, such as 2013 and 2014, the change in the *volume* of expenditures on domestically produced goods and services. To do this, expenditure in the most recent year (e.g. 2014) is re-estimated as if price levels in the previous year (e.g. 2013) had continued.

When the first step is complete, we have a series showing the percentage change in the volume of expenditures from year to year. The second step then involves choosing a *base year*, say 2009. Starting from the nominal GDP value in the base year, the percentage changes in volumes previously calculated are applied. The resulting series is our real GDP series.

The value of the real GDP series in the base year is the same as nominal GDP. The percentage changes in the real GDP series represent the change in the volume of output. If we were to change the base year, the real values of the series would change, but the percentage changes from year to year would remain the same.

Key definition

Chain linking

The process of applying estimates of the percentage change in the volume of output between consecutive years to the nominal GDP series starting from a chosen base year.

When monitoring economic growth we are comparing real GDP from period to period. Economic growth, therefore, measures the change in the level of real GDP. You will often find economic commentators reporting on economic growth, especially when the latest 'official' figures on growth are released. Typically, they are reporting on economic growth over short periods of time. Commonly, economists compare real GDP over 3-month and 12-month periods. These are measures of **short-term economic growth**.

Figure 1.1 plots the annual rate of change in real GDP. From it, we can see the considerable variations in the rates of economic growth. This is a common feature of developed economies. The variability of economic growth gives rise to the concept of the **business cycle**. The business cycle encapsulates the volatility of economies. If the rates of economic growth were constant then the level of real GDP would grow smoothly.

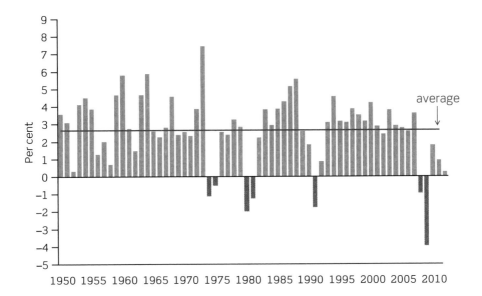

Figure 1.1 Annual rates of economic growth in the UK.

Source: Based on data from *Quarterly National Accounts*, National Statistics (Series ABMI).

Assessment advice

As you go through most of the chapters, you will see reminders of the importance of being aware of general patterns and trends in relevant economic data. This awareness can help to support your understanding of economic concepts and theories. You do not need to be a 'data junkie'. Rather, you need to be able to demonstrate a general awareness of the real world that we are trying to understand. In the current context, an awareness of the patterns in economic growth in the UK (and other countries) would be an advantage.

As well as analysing growth over the short term, economists analyse the rate of economic growth over much longer periods of time, perhaps generations. By measuring the average rate of growth in real GDP over many years we get a sense of **long-term economic growth** and, hence, of the rate of economic development. In the UK, the average (mean) rate of growth in real GDP since the 1950s has been of the order of 2½ per cent per year. This is shown in Figure 1.1 alongside the actual annual rates of economic growth.

Key definitions

Short-term economic growth

The change in real GDP over short periods of time. Commonly, short-term economic growth is measured over 3 months or 12 months.

Business cycle

The fluctuations in real GDP that result from variations in short-term rates of economic growth.

Long-term economic growth

The change in real GDP over an extended period of time, perhaps over several generations.

Comparing GDP across countries

As well as comparing a country's GDP over time, we often want to compare GDP across countries. This requires comparing GDP figures presented in local currency, such as in British pounds or US dollars. If we want to compare *growth rates* across countries then we can simply compare percentage changes. A problem arises when we want to compare the *levels* of GDP in different countries. How can we compare the relative size of the two economies, for example the UK and USA?

One approach to comparing the size of economies is to use published exchange rates and present different countries' GDP figures in a *common currency*, say the US dollar. However, this approach can give misleading results when current exchange rates are poor indicators of currencies' purchasing power.

Assume that in the UK an individual exchanges an amount of British pounds for US dollars. This amount of British pounds allows the individual to purchase a particular basket of goods and services in the UK. Assume too that the exchange rate is $2 = £1 (2 US dollars to 1 British pound). This is the US price of the British pound.

Our individual now travels to the USA. There the individual finds their amount of dollars buys the same basket of goods but with cash to spare. This means that the US dollar is undervalued (the British pound overvalued). The actual exchange rate underestimates the purchasing power of the US dollar (overestimates the value of the British pound). The US price of the British pound is too high to ensure purchasing-power parity between the USA and the UK.

If the US dollar is undervalued, then, when we convert British GDP into US dollar equivalents, we overestimate the purchasing power of British national income and underestimate the purchasing power of US national income. Put another way, we would be overstating the size of the British economy relative to the US economy.

To overcome the problem of actual exchange rates inaccurately reflecting purchasing power, estimates of countries' GDP are converted into a common currency at a **purchasing-power parity exchange rate**. In our example, this would be at a lower US dollar price of the British pound; that is, where £1 purchases fewer US dollars. The adjustment would be such that the (lower) amount of US dollars bought by a given amount of British pounds would be just enough to purchase the same basket of goods over in the USA.

 Assessment advice

Take care not to be confused by alternative presentations of exchange rates. Here we have used *the foreign currency price of the domestic currency*. For example, the foreign currency price of the British pound could be the number of euros per £1, Swiss francs per £1 or US dollars per £1.

Another important consideration when comparing the size of economies is the size of the population or the size of the workforce. The UK has a population of just over 60 million compared with 315 million in the USA. Therefore, if we want to say something meaningful about living standards in the two economies it is preferable to compare GDP per person, commonly referred to as **GDP per capita**, rather than the level of GDP.

Purchasing-power parity exchange rate
The exchange rate that allows a given amount of money in one country to buy the same amount of goods in another country using the currency of the other country.

GDP per capita
GDP per head of the population.

Figure 1.2 brings together the concepts of purchasing-power parity (PPP) and GDP per capita. It shows the level of GDP per capita in PPP US dollars for a selection of countries in 2012. The ranking of countries is also shown. Qatar has the highest PPP per capita GDP and the UK is ranked 22nd.

Based on PPP GDP, rather than PPP GDP per capita, the USA is ranked 1st, China 2nd, the UK 8th and Qatar 57th. In the example on pages 11–12, we consider the ranking of countries under the Human Development Index (HDI). Although it takes into account economic development, the HDI is a more broadly based measure of overall human development.

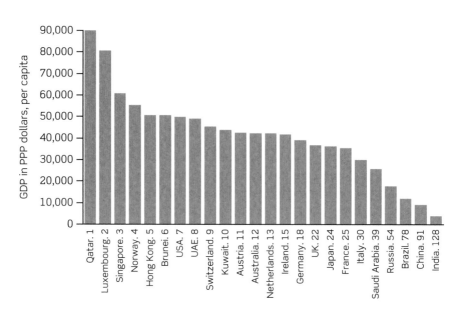

Figure 1.2 GDP in PPP dollars, per capita, 2012.
Note: 2012 figures are forecasts.
Source: Based on data from *World Economic Outlook*, IMF.

Examples & evidence

Human Development Index

GDP is an imperfect measure of economic development. A more broadly based measure of human development is the Human Development Index (HDI), published annually by the United Nations Development Programme (UNDP). The HDI captures three *dimensions* of development: life expectancy at birth, access to education (incorporating both adult literacy and years of schooling) and real gross national income per capita in US dollars at PPP exchange rates.

Indices are created for each dimension with values (goalposts) varying between 0 (minimum) and 1 (maximum). The overall HDI index is then an average of the three individual indices. Finally, countries are categorised as displaying very high human development (0.9 to 1.0), high human development (0.8 to 0.899), medium human development (0.5 to 0.799) and low human development (below 0.5).

Table 1.1 shows the HDI for 2011 along with other evidence relating to the three dimensions of development. The final column shows the difference between the global ranking based on gross national income and the ranking based on the HDI. The UK had the 28th highest HDI ranking. Its HDI of 0.863 means that it displays *high* human development. When ranked by gross national income the UK is 21st. From this, we might infer that gross national income overstates the UK's level of human development.

Table 1.1

HDI rank	Country	HDI	Life expectancy at birth (years)	Mean years of schooling (years)	GNY per capita (constant 2005 prices, US$ PPP)	GNY per capita rank minus HDI rank
1	Norway	0.943	81.1	12.6	47,557	6
2	Australia	0.929	81.9	12.0	34,431	16
3	Netherlands	0.910	80.7	11.6	36,402	9
4	United States	0.910	78.5	12.4	43,017	6
5	New Zealand	0.908	80.7	12.5	23,737	30

HDI rank	Country	HDI	Life expectancy at birth (years)	Mean years of schooling (years)	GNY per capita (constant 2005 prices, US$ PPP)	GNY per capita rank minus HDI rank
28	UK	0.863	80.2	9.3	33,296	−7
183	Chad	0.328	49.6	1.5	1,105	−12
184	Mozambique	0.322	50.2	1.2	898	−9
185	Burundi	0.316	50.4	2.7	368	0
186	Niger	0.295	54.7	1.4	641	−4
187	Democratic Republic of the Congo	0.286	48.4	3.5	280	−1

Source: Based on data from *Human Development Report*, 2011, United Nations Development Programme.

Questions

1. What are the advantages and disadvantages of using GDP as a measure of economic development?

2. What does a negative value in the last column of Table 1.1 indicate? What about a positive value?

Other macroeconomic indicators

Inflation

Inflation refers to rising price levels and deflation refers to falling price levels. The rate of inflation (deflation) is the rate at which price levels are rising (falling). Rates of inflation (deflation) are typically calculated over a 12-month period, in which case we refer to the **annual rate of inflation** (deflation).

Key definitions

Inflation

A rise in the *level* of prices.

Annual rate of inflation

The *percentage increase* in the level of prices over a 12-month period.

We come face to face with all sorts of prices, such as the price of a loaf of a bread, the price of a litre of petrol, the price of residential housing and the price paid (wage) for employing staff. Therefore, it is possible to calculate rates of inflation for various types of goods and services. In macroeconomics, because we focus on broad aggregates, we are interested in the average price levels of broad groupings of goods and services. We have already encountered one aggregate price level: the GDP deflator. This is a measure of the price of all domestically produced goods and services.

Arguably, the best-known measure of inflation is the annual Consumer Price Index (CPI) inflation rate. It measures the annual rate of increase in the CPI. The CPI tracks the average price of a basket of everyday goods and services. The basket is updated annually to reflect changes in consumption patterns. The annual CPI inflation rate in the UK since 1989 is shown in Figure 1.3.

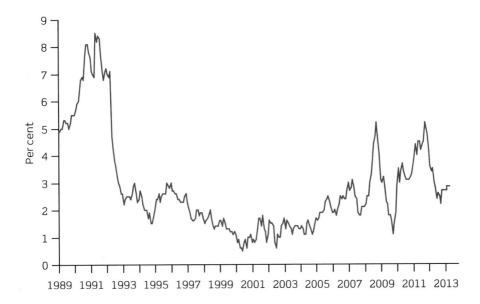

Figure 1.3 Annual rates of CPI inflation in the UK.

Source: Consumer Price Indices, National Statistics (Series D7G7).

The Bank of England is charged by the UK government to meet a symmetrical CPI inflation rate target of 2 per cent (the central target) plus or minus 1 per cent. The Monetary Policy Committee (MPC) meets monthly to decide on the interest rate (bank rate) at which the Bank of England is prepared to lend to banks. In this way, it can then influence interest rates set by commercial banks. The Bank then hopes that changes in interest rates will affect the public's total demand for goods and services and, in turn, the rate at which prices change. The total demand for an economy's goods and services is known as **aggregate demand**. By altering the bank rate, the Bank of England looks to affect the level of aggregate demand.

Key definition

Aggregate demand

The total level of spending on goods and services made in the economy.

Recap

Inflation refers to an increase in price levels. Macroeconomists focus on increases in aggregate price measures such as the GDP deflator and the Consumer Price Index (CPI). An annual rate of inflation measures the percentage change in the price level over a 12-month period. The annual CPI inflation rate is perhaps the best-known inflation rate and is the inflation rate that the Bank of England targets.

Test yourself

Q1. Would an increase in consumer prices lead to an increase in the rate of consumer price inflation?

Q2. Draw up a list of the different inflation rates with which you are familiar. Would you expect these different inflation rates to tend to move together?

✱ Assessment advice

A common confusion surrounds the distinction between price levels and rates of inflation. Try, by drawing on actual examples, to illustrate clearly this distinction.

Unemployment

The internationally agreed measure of unemployment is someone who is available to start work within two weeks and who has been actively seeking work. When expressed as a percentage of the workforce of working age (i.e. those either unemployed or employed), we derive the **standardised unemployment rate**. Figure 1.4 allows us to track the standardised unemployment rate for the UK since 1971.

Most countries also publish unemployment statistics based on the entitlement to welfare. In the UK, this measure is the **claimant count**. However, because entitlement conditions can vary across time and between countries, the standardised measure is generally the preferred measure amongst economists.

Key definitions

Standardised unemployment rate

The percentage of the workforce of working age without work who are available for work and are actively seeking employment.

Claimant count

An administrative measure of unemployment based on those entitled to the 'Jobseeker's Allowance'.

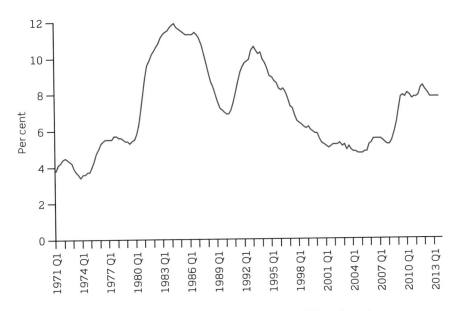

Figure 1.4 UK standardised unemployment rate (%) (aged 16 and over).

Source: Labour Market Statistics, National Statistics (Series MGSX).

Later, we will focus more closely on the issue of unemployment and its causes (see Chapter 6). However, economists tend to distinguish between **equilibrium unemployment** and **disequilibrium unemployment**. This distinction relates to the market for labour (workers). Disequilibrium unemployment occurs when the average *real* wage is above equilibrium. The average real wage is the average nominal (actual) wage adjusted for the average price of consumer goods and services. This allows us to measure workers' purchasing power. When disequilibrium unemployment occurs, the aggregate supply of labour is greater than the aggregate demand for labour.

In reality, the *aggregate* labour market comprises a series of labour markets. We could distinguish, for instance, between labour markets based on geography or different industrial sectors. Equilibrium unemployment occurs when individual markets are in disequilibrium, despite the aggregate demand for labour being equal to the aggregate supply of labour. This could mean that particular regions of the country or sectors of the economy are experiencing an excess supply of labour while, at the same time, other regions or sectors are experiencing excess demand.

Key definitions

Disequilibrium unemployment

Unemployment that results from real wages being above the equilibrium level.

Equilibrium unemployment

The difference between those willing to take employment at current wage rates and those actually able to.

Recap

The unemployment rate measures the percentage of the labour force that is unemployed. Economists most frequently use the standardised unemployment rate when making historical or international comparisons. Economic theory helps us to distinguish between equilibrium and disequilibrium unemployment.

Test yourself

Q1. Why is the *standardised rate* of *unemployment* higher than the claimant count rate of unemployment?

Q2. How might the level of equilibrium unemployment be affected by a country's changing industrial composition?

Balance of payments

The **balance of payments** is a record of all transactions that occur between countries. There are three separate accounts. The first is the **current account**. It records the money flows arising from the import and export of goods and services, income flows arising from profits, wages and interest income and the transfers of income between economic agents in different countries for the purpose of consumption (i.e. current transfers).

The second, and the smallest by value, is the **capital account**. It records cross-border transactions involving the acquisition or disposal of non-produced, non-financial assets, including rights to natural resources, copyright and patents, and the transfers of income for the purposes of investment (i.e. capital transfers).

The third account is the **financial account**. It records transactions involving financial assets and liabilities. These range from significant cross-border investments or disinvestments in companies, trading in shares or debt instruments (e.g. commercial or government bonds) or deposits or loans involving foreign financial institutions.

Key definitions

Balance of payments
A record of all of a country's transactions with the rest of the world.

Current account
The balance of trade in goods and services, plus net income flows and current transfers of money.

Capital account
A record of the transfer of ownership of non-produced, non-financial assets and of capital transfers.

Financial account
A record of cross-border transactions involving financial instruments, such as deposits with financial institutions.

We will look at the balance of payments in more detail later (see Chapter 7). However, it is worth noting here that commentators pay considerable attention to the trade in goods and services. This is the most significant part of the current account and is the record of cross-border transactions in goods and services. From it, we can calculate a country's **balance of trade**. When a country exports more goods and services than it imports, it runs a balance of trade surplus. If it imports more than it exports, the country runs a balance of trade deficit.

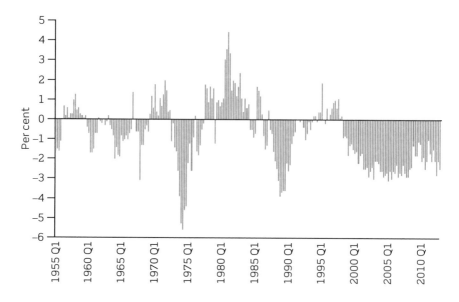

Figure 1.5 UK balance of trade, percentage of GDP.

Source: Balance of Payments quarterly First Release, National Statistics (Series D28L).

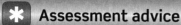

Key definition

Balance of trade (in goods and services)

The balance between a country's exports and imports in goods and services.

Figure 1.5 shows the UK's balance of trade as a percentage of GDP since the mid-1950s. Since the mid-1980s, the UK has consistently run a balance of trade deficit.

It is important not to confuse the terms *balance of trade* and *balance of payments*. The balance of trade is only one part of the overall balance of payments. As we have just seen, there are other transactions that occur between countries. Therefore, only the balance of payments is a complete record of all cross-border transactions.

✱ Assessment advice

Take care not to confuse the concepts of *balance of trade* and *balance of payments*. The balance of trade is a component part of the balance of payments.

Cross-border transactions affect the demand and supply of currencies and can therefore affect exchange rates. For example, when UK residents want to buy goods and services from abroad or want to invest abroad they create a supply of pounds on the foreign exchange market. On the other hand, when foreign residents want to purchase UK goods and services or invest in the UK they create a demand for pounds on the foreign exchange market. The rates of exchange between currencies will reflect the demands for and supplies of currencies on the foreign exchange market.

Recap

The balance of payments is a record of cross-border transactions. It comprises the current account, capital account and the financial account. Considerable attention is focused on the balance of trade in goods and services. The UK has consistently run a balance of trade deficit since the mid-1980s. Cross-border transactions create a demand for and a supply of currencies on the foreign exchange market.

Test yourself

Q1. What does the balance of trade record?

Q2. Does a deterioration of the balance of trade mean a deterioration of the balance of payments?

Although we have so far considered the macroeconomic indicators separately, they can and do move together. For instance, an increase in the rate of economic growth, say following a strengthening of aggregate demand, might be accompanied by higher rates of inflation, lower rates of unemployment and a worsening balance of trade as more imports are consumed.

In the following chapters, we will look at these four key macroeconomic variables in more detail. In particular, we will try to understand what causes them to behave in the way they do. To understand their determinants better we will look at some of the alternative explanations proposed by economists.

The role of government

Government intervention

An area of considerable debate among economists is the role that governments should play in economies. Some economists advocate a 'pro-market' approach, leaving economic decision making predominantly to individuals.

Other economists favour a more interventionist approach with governments actively intervening to try to affect economic outcomes.

By intervening in the economy, the government can induce two principal types of effects:

- *Allocative effects*. Through its policy choices, government may affect the *allocation* of resources. This means that it affects the consumption and production decisions of economic agents. For instance, governments may attempt to affect the aggregate level of spending or saving by households.

- *Distributive effects*. The government may use policy to affect the distribution of resources. For instance, it may look to affect the distribution of incomes or to make certain goods and services more widely available than might otherwise be the case.

In macroeconomics, we are interested in how these effects impact on the economy and, of course, our four key macroeconomic variables. In other words, we are interested in the macroeconomic impact of governments' policy choices. We tend to distinguish between their short-term and long-term impact.

In the context of the short term, macroeconomists are particularly interested in the role that governments play in affecting the business cycle. As we saw earlier, the business cycle refers to the fluctuations in real GDP resulting from the variability in short-term rates of economic growth. Some economists argue that, because the economy is so inherently volatile, governments ought to play an active role in trying to reduce this volatility. Therefore, through its policy choices government should try to stabilise the economy. In contrast, other economists believe that government intervention may actually make the fluctuations in real GDP larger.

Macroeconomists also debate the long-term impact of governments' policy choices on the economy. Of particular importance is the long-term rate of economic growth of the economy. What role should governments play in helping to foster economic development over the generations? Again, economists favour either a more 'pro-market' approach or a more interventionist approach.

Fiscal and monetary policy

We now consider the policy instruments available to government and/or the central bank. We can distinguish between two types of policy: fiscal policy and monetary policy.

Fiscal policy refers to changes by government in its level of spending and/or rates of taxation. An expansionary fiscal policy (a 'looser' fiscal policy) involves either an increase in government spending or a decrease in taxation. A contractionary fiscal policy involves either a reduction in government spending or an increase in taxation. A deliberate change in government spending and/or tax rates is known as **discretionary fiscal policy**.

Key definitions

Fiscal policy
Changes in the level of government spending and/or rates of taxation.

Discretionary fiscal policy
Deliberate changes in the level of government spending and/or rates of taxation.

Spending by the UK public sector (government and public corporations) has frequently exceeded its receipts. The deficit is known as **public-sector net borrowing** (PSNB). Figure 1.6 tracks public-sector net borrowing and the stock of public-sector debt.

Key definition

Public-sector net borrowing (PSNB)
The difference between the expenditures of the public sector and its receipts from taxation and other revenues from public corporations.

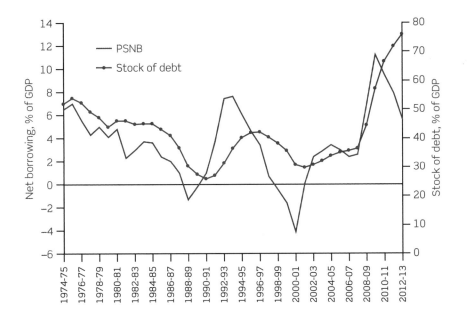

Figure 1.6 Public-sector net borrowing and stock of debt as a percentage of GDP.
Source: Public Sector Finances Databank, HM Treasury.

Public-sector net borrowing is measured here as a percentage of GDP (left-hand axis). The average deficit since (financial year) 1974–5 has been equivalent to 3½ per cent of GDP. In 2009–10, following the financial crisis and subsequent economic downturn, the UK deficit exceeded 11 per cent of GDP. This period marked a period of greater intervention by the authorities in order to stabilise the financial system and to attempt to limit the economic downturn (see Figure 1.1). The early 2010s, however, saw a tightening of fiscal policy as the government attempted to reduce borrowing. The pace of this tightening divided economic (and political) opinion.

Figure 1.6 also tracks the stock of public-sector debt as a percentage of GDP (right-hand axis). The public sector accumulates debt when it borrows funds by issuing debt. In the UK, short-term government debt instruments are Treasury bills and longer-term debt instruments are gilts (bonds). They are both examples of financial IOUs. When the public sector runs a budget surplus, it is able to repay debt. From 2008–9, the sector's stock of debt rose sharply as a percentage of GDP. In 2012–13, the debt-to-GDP ratio reached 75 per cent.

 Assessment advice

Avoid confusing your *stocks* and *flows*! Borrowing is a *flow* concept. If over a given period, say a calendar month, the flow of government spending is greater than the flow of receipts (largely taxation), then the government will need to borrow. It will borrow by issuing debt. Consequently, this flow of borrowing will add to the government's existing *stock* of debt.

Monetary policy involves the central bank affecting the quantity or price of money. In many countries today, including the UK, monetary policy involves the central bank influencing the structure of interest rates in the economy.

Key definition

Monetary policy

Actions taken by the authorities to affect the quantity or price of money.

Since May 1997, the Bank of England has set interest rates to meet an inflation rate target set by the government. It has independence to determine the bank rate and, hence, the rate at which it will lend central bank money to financial institutions. It is the Bank of England's short-term lending rate. Figure 1.7 tracks the level of the bank rate since the start of 1997.

As we saw earlier, changes in the bank rate affect other interest rates in the economy, including, for instance, mortgage rates. This is because changes in the bank rate affect the rate at which financial institutions can borrow

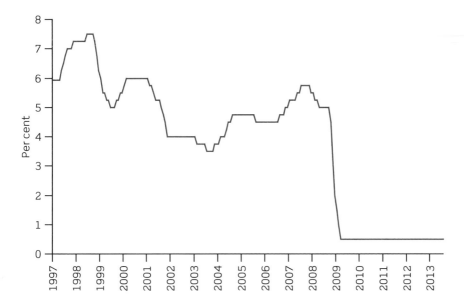

Figure 1.7 Bank rate, end of month (%).

Source: Statistical Interactive Database, Bank of England (Series IUMBEDR).

short-term funds from the Bank of England. Changes in the structure of interest rates in the economy should then affect the level of aggregate demand and, consequently, the rate of price inflation.

Recap

Fiscal policy relates to changes in the level of government spending and/or rates of taxation. The UK public sector (government and public corporations) has typically run deficits and therefore has accumulated a stock of debt. Monetary policy relates to changes in the quantity and/or price of money. The Bank of England meets monthly to decide on the bank rate. It provides short-term lending for financial institutions at this rate.

Test yourself

Fill in the blanks below:

When government tightens fiscal policy it _____ spending and/or _____ taxes. When the central bank tightens monetary policy it _____ the bank rate. A tightening of fiscal policy and/or monetary policy would be expected to _____ aggregate demand and _____ the rate of inflation. Meanwhile, the rate of economic growth might _____, while the rate of unemployment _____.

Chapter summary – pulling it all together

By the end of this chapter you should be able to:

	Confident ✓	Not confident?
Explain with examples the distinction between micro- and macroeconomic analysis		Revise pages 2–3
Identify alternative measures of the size of the economy		Revise pages 3–5
Explain the distinction between nominal and real GDP		Revise pages 5–7
Explain what economists mean by economic growth		Revise pages 7–8
Explain what is meant by purchasing-power parity and its importance when comparing GDP across countries		Revise pages 8–10
Define inflation and the rate of inflation, and identify commonly referred-to measures of inflation		Revise pages 12–14
Define the terms unemployment and the rate of unemployment		Revise pages 15–16
Distinguish between equilibrium and disequilibrium unemployment		Revise page 16
Explain what is recorded by the balance of payments and distinguish it from the balance of trade		Revise pages 17–19
Explain what is meant by the allocative and distributive effects of government policy		Revise pages 19–20
Explain what is meant by fiscal and monetary policy		Revise pages 20–23

Now try the assessment question at the start of this chapter, using the answer guidelines below.

Answer guidelines

✳ Assessment question

With reference to real-world examples, describe some of the key issues analysed by macroeconomists.

Approaching the question

The question is inviting you to draw out the distinction between micro- and macroeconomic analysis with reference to real-world issues.

Important points to include

- **Distinction between micro- and macroeconomic analysis**. Explain how the focus of the two principal branches of economics differs.

- **Key macroeconomic issues**. Identify the key macroeconomic indicators including: economic growth, inflation, unemployment, the balance of payments and the role that government might be expected to play.

- **Definitions**. In exploring each of the issues, be sure to define carefully and accurately the related concepts, for example real GDP in the case of economic growth.

Make your answer stand out

- Try to avoid simply *listing* macroeconomic issues. Show your understanding by drawing on real-world examples, thereby illustrating your awareness of the macroeconomic environment.

- Try to incorporate a range of contemporary examples relating to the four general issues, but if possible drawing on other macroeconomic issues too – for example, issues around government borrowing and the eurozone crisis. Again, the aim is to show your awareness of the macroeconomic environment and current events. Therefore, try to relate to macroeconomic stories that have been in the news.

- Try and draw out historical and international comparisons wherever possible.

Read to impress

Here are some books, articles and other sources that you can use to develop your answers on the topic area.

Books

Griffiths, A. and Wall, S. (2011) *Economics for Business and Management*, 3rd edition, Chapter 9, 'National income determination'. Harlow, UK: Pearson Education.

Parkin, M., Powell, M. and Matthews, K. (2012) *Essential Economics*, European edition, Chapter 10, 'Real GDP'. Harlow, UK: Pearson Education.

Parkin, M., Powell, M. and Matthews, K. (2012) *Essential Economics*, European edition, Chapter 11, 'Monitoring jobs and inflation'. Harlow, UK: Pearson Education.

Sloman, J. and Garratt, D. (2013) *Essentials of Economics*, 6th edition, Chapter 8, 'National economy'. Harlow, UK: Pearson Education.

Articles

Lee, P. (2011) UK national accounts – a short guide. Office for National Statistics, London.

Hills, S., Thomas, R. and Dimsdale, N. (2010) UK recession in context – what do three centuries of data tell us? *Bank of England Quarterly Bulletin*, Q4: 277–90 (www.bankofengland.co.uk/publications /Documents/quarterlybulletin/qb100403.pdf).

Joyce, M., Tong, M. and Woods, R. (2011) The United Kingdom's quantitative easing policy: design, operation and impact. *Bank of England Quarterly Bulletin*, Q3: 200–12 (www.bankofengland.co.uk /publications/Documents/quarterlybulletin/qb110301.pdf).

Periodicals and newspapers

The Bank of England's *Inflation Report* contains a readable overview of recent patterns in the national economy.

HM Treasury Budget documents provide an overview of the current state of the national and global economies, economic forecasts and details of fiscal policy announcements (www.hm-treasury.gov.uk/budget.htm).

The *Office for National Statistics* publishes a range of relevant data and supporting commentaries on the economy. These include releases relating to the following:

National income, expenditure and output: www.ons.gov.uk/ons
/taxonomy/index.html?nscl=National+Income%2C+Expenditure+and
+Output

Unemployment: www.ons.gov.uk/ons/taxonomy/index.
html?nscl=Labour+Market

Inflation: www.ons.gov.uk/ons/taxonomy/index.html?nscl=Price+Indices
+and+Inflation

Balance of payments: www.ons.gov.uk/ons/taxonomy/index.
html?nscl=Balance+of+Payments

BBC News (2013) David Cameron: Cheap borrowing the priority. 6 January.

Financial Times (2012) UK trade deficit widens in April. Norma Cohen,
15 June.

Financial Times (2012) Air fares lift UK inflation to 2.6%. Norma Cohen,
14 August.

Financial Times (2012) IMF forecast leaves chancellor in a fix. Chris Giles,
9 October.

Financial Times (2012) US jobless claims drop sharply to 339,000. Anjil
Raval, 11 October.

Financial Times (2012) Blow for Osborne as borrowing rises. Chris Giles
and Claire Jones, 21 December.

Financial Times (2012) GDP growth revised down to 0.9%. Claire Jones,
21 December.

Companion website

Go to the companion website at **www.pearsoned.co.uk/econexpress** to
find more revision support online for this topic area.

Notes

2 Aggregate demand and national income

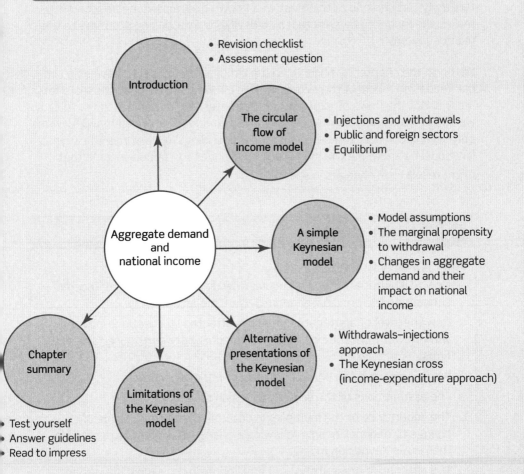

- Revision checklist
- Assessment question

Introduction

The circular flow of income model
- Injections and withdrawals
- Public and foreign sectors
- Equilibrium

Aggregate demand and national income

A simple Keynesian model
- Model assumptions
- The marginal propensity to withdrawal
- Changes in aggregate demand and their impact on national income

Alternative presentations of the Keynesian model
- Withdrawals–injections approach
- The Keynesian cross (income-expenditure approach)

Chapter summary

Limitations of the Keynesian model

- Test yourself
- Answer guidelines
- Read to impress

A printable version of this topic map is available from **www.pearsoned.co.uk/econexpress**

Introduction

One of the most fundamental questions macroeconomists and policy-makers face is by how much an economy will grow over the coming months and quarters. What we would like to determine is the level of national income both now and at a point in the near future. By doing so we could say something about *short-term* economic growth.

In this chapter, we look at how the size of the economy might be affected by the total demand for the good and services of firms in an economy, that is the economy's aggregate demand. To do so we introduce the *circular flow of income model* which enables us to identify the *sources* of demands for firms' output and, consequently, how the flows of *expenditures* received by firms may rise or fall. The fact that the model can be illustrated relatively straightforwardly through one of the most well-known diagrams in macroeconomics makes the model a powerful teaching device for introducing students to the macroeconomy.

We finish the chapter by building on the circular flow model to develop a simple *Keynesian model* of the economy. This allows us to think a little more formally about the flows of expenditure that determine national income. To do so we analyse the components of aggregate demand (the total demand for firms' output) and consider the determinants of spending. We conclude the Keynesian model by analysing the magnitude of changes to national income that might result from changes in spending.

 ## Revision checklist

What you need to know:

- ❑ How to illustrate through a 'circular flow diagram' the flows of income connecting the principal economic agents in an economy.
- ❑ How the level of aggregate demand is affected by injections into and withdrawals from the circular flow of income between households and firms.
- ❑ What is meant by an equilibrium level of national income.
- ❑ The assumptions of the simple Keynesian model.
- ❑ The importance of the multiplier in determining the magnitude of change to national income following a change in aggregate demand in the simple Keynesian model.
- ❑ The alternative presentations of equilibrium in the simple Keynesian model.

Assessment question

Can you answer this essay-type question? Guidelines on answering the question are presented at the end of this chapter.

With the aid of a diagram, describe the income flows in the circular flow of income model. Using a simple Keynesian model, discuss the impact on national income of a *reduction* in injections into the circular flow.

The circular flow of income model

The acts of consumption and production are the fundamental activities in an economy. Consequently, when beginning to model an economy we identify two groups (also known as sectors): households and firms. The two sectors are interdependent with both flows of goods and services and payments for these goods and services connecting them. This is illustrated in Figure 2.1.

On the left-hand side, we can see how in return for households supplying land, labour and capital they receive incomes in the form of wages and salaries, dividends and shares, interest payments and rent. These incomes are collectively

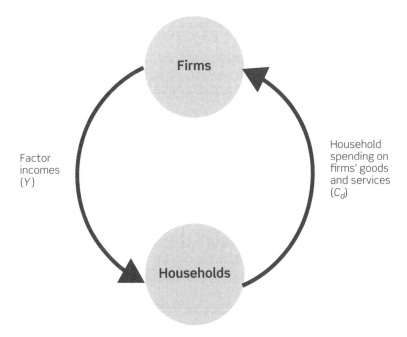

Figure 2.1 Circular flow of income: households and firms.

known as **factor incomes** (Y). On the right-hand side, we can see the flow of income resulting from household consumption on domestically produced goods and services (C_d).

We assume that prices are constant. Therefore, in the absence of inflation, a change in the flow of factor payments represents a change in the level of output. Similarly, in the absence of inflation, a change in spending by households represents a change in the volume of demand for firms' goods and services. The total demand for domestically produced goods and services is known as **aggregate demand**.

Key definitions

Factor incomes

Incomes that result from the services provided by the factors of production.

Aggregate demand

The total level of spending on goods and services made in the economy.

Recap

The simplest version of the circular flow of income model focuses on the income flows between an economy's households and firms.

Test yourself

Q1. What are the *incomes* flowing from firms to households and from households to firms?

Q2. What are the physical goods and services flowing between households and firms?

Injections and withdrawals

As we saw earlier (Chapter 1), the level of economic activity (real GDP) is constantly changing. So, how can we apply the circular flow model to fit these facts? Actually, we need to do two things. First, we need to recognise that the flow of incomes passing between households and firms changes. Second – and this is the key – we need to recognise that there are **injections** into and **withdrawals** from the core of our model that affect the flow of income passing between households and firms. Therefore, the total demand for firms' goods and services changes. This means that aggregate demand changes and, as a consequence, the level of output changes. The size of the economy is therefore determined by the level of aggregate demand: the total flow of income into firms.

Key definitions

Injections

Spending on firms' goods and services by purchasers other than domestic households.

Withdrawals (or leakages)

Incomes of domestic households or firms that leak out of the inner flow between households and firms.

An injection into our circular flow represents *additional* income available to our firms that did not come directly from our households. In other words, it is income that does not come from the inner flow between domestic households and domestic firms. Conversely, a withdrawal (also referred to as a leakage) represents a *reduction* in income directly flowing to firms in the economy because income is not being passed around the inner flow.

With only households and firms in our model we can identify one injection and one withdrawal. Consider Figure 2.2. The injection is *investment* (I). Firms also purchase final goods and services. However, these purchases are physical

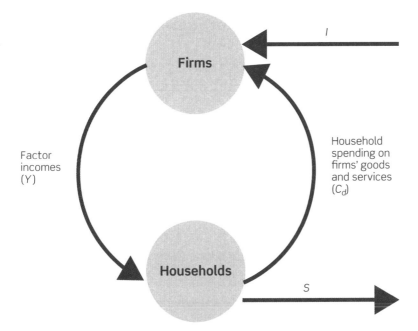

Figure 2.2 Circular flow of income incorporating saving and investment.

assets that are used by firms to help produce goods and services. Machinery is one such example. A greater flow of investment expenditure, all other things remaining equal, means a larger aggregate level of expenditure on firms' goods and services. Aggregate demand rises and the economy grows.

The withdrawal is *saving*. Saving is income that households choose not to spend. In fact, when thinking about saving we need to recognise that households can actually increase their current spending by drawing on past savings or by borrowing. So, it is more accurate to refer to our withdrawal as *net saving* (*S*).

The greater the level of net saving, the smaller the flow of income being directly returned to firms by households and, all other things being equal, the lower the aggregate level of expenditure on firms' goods and services. An increase in net saving results in aggregate demand falling and the economy contracting.

Recap

Injections are income flows to firms that arise from outside the 'inner flow' between households and firms. Withdrawals (or leakages) are income flows that leave the 'inner flow'. In the two-sector circular flow model, the injection is investment (*I*) and the withdrawal is net saving (*S*).

Test yourself

Q1. What impact does an increase in the amount of credit extended by financial institutions have on aggregate demand? Does this reflect a change in injections or withdrawals?

Q2. What types of expenditure would be included under investment (*I*)?

At this point, you may have recognised another important sector of the economy: the financial system. Financial institutions act as the intermediary between those with income to save and those who need to borrow to supplement current incomes. This explains why some representations of the circular flow model show financial institutions channelling the net savings of the household sector to fund the investment expenditure of firms. Although this is a simplistic representation of the role that financial institutions play, it does demonstrate how financial institutions can and do affect the level of aggregate demand.

✳ Assessment advice

It is important that you demonstrate an awareness not only of the sources of income flows to firms, but also of how they can affect the level of aggregate demand and, in turn, the size of the economy.

Public and foreign sectors

A major 'player' in the economy is the public sector. Some corporations are publicly owned; that is, owned by the state. This can be readily incorporated into our existing model by simply treating firms, regardless of ownership, as comprising a single sector: the corporate sector. The rest of the public sector is known as **general government**. This comprises local and central government. General government is a purchaser of firms' goods and services in delivering public services, such as education and health care. Government purchases (G) are an injection into the inner flow of income. Increased government purchases, other things remaining equal, increase the level of aggregate demand and so increase the level of national income.

Key definition

General government
The collective name for local and central government.

Government needs to fund its purchases, and to do so it levies taxes. The payment of taxes represents a withdrawal from the incomes flowing between households and firms. Taxes may be levied on these incomes, for example on the profits of firms (corporation tax) or on employment income (income tax and social security contributions). Alternatively, taxes can be levied on consumption through excise duties on specific products or through a more generally applied sales tax (e.g. VAT in the UK).

It is customary in the circular flow diagram to show taxation as a single withdrawal reducing the income that households have available for consumption. This abstraction from the complexities of modern tax systems does not affect the main point that households are able to purchase fewer consumption goods and services as a result of taxation.

Income also flows from government to households. Some of this is the payment by government to those employed to run public services, such as teachers, nurses and civil servants. But a sizeable proportion is the payment of benefits, such as unemployment benefits and pensions. These are also known as transfer payments because income is being transferred from taxpayers to the recipients of the benefits. To accommodate these flows to households we refer to the withdrawal as *net taxation* (NT). An increase in net taxation reduces aggregate demand and, as a consequence, the output of firms.

The final sector to be introduced into our model is the *foreign sector*. Globalisation has seen an increased interconnectedness between economies as nations trade goods and services. The withdrawal that results from trade is *imports* (M). Some of the purchases made by households, firms and government involve goods and services that are made in part or in whole overseas. As a result, income flows to foreign producers. Import expenditures (M), therefore, involve a withdrawal of income away from domestic producers. An increase in imports will, other things remaining constant, reduce aggregate demand and thus the output of firms.

In contrast, expenditures on domestically produced goods and services made by foreign households, firms and government are a flow of income to domestic firms. Exports (X) are therefore an injection. An increase in exports will, other things remaining constant, increase aggregate demand and increase output.

A simplified version of the circular flow model incorporating all four sectors (households, firms, government and the overseas sector) and all injections (I, G and X) and all withdrawals (S, NT and M) is shown in Figure 2.3.

Recap

The four-sector circular flow of income model incorporates domestic households, firms and government along with their foreign counterparts overseas. In the four-sector model, the injections are investment, government purchases and exports, and the withdrawals are net saving, net taxation and imports.

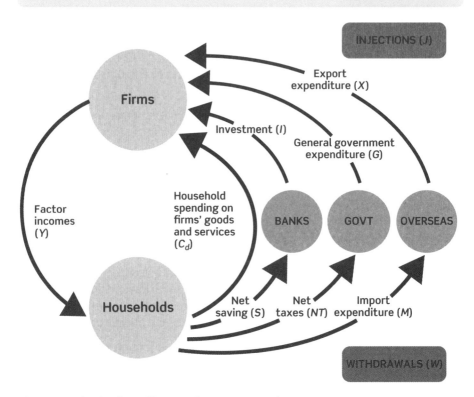

Figure 2.3 Circular flow of income: four-sector version.

Test yourself

Fill in the blanks in the following:

An increase in the levels of benefits paid by government to the household sector _____ the level of net taxation. As a result, this _____ from the circular flow of income _____ and aggregate demand _____. In response to this _____ in aggregate demand, firms _____ output and national income _____.

Equilibrium

Equilibrium in the circular flow of income model occurs when the total flow of income received by domestic firms (aggregate demand) is exactly matched by the flow of income paid out by these firms to households (Y).

Another way of thinking about the equilibrium level of national income is to recognise that for the flows of income to and from firms to remain constant, the injections (J) into the circular flow need to be matched by the withdrawals (W) from the circular flow. This means that the equilibrium national level of national income is that at which the sum of injections ($I + G + X$) equals the sum of withdrawals ($S + NT + M$).

✳ Assessment advice

A common mistake is to think that equilibrium requires investment spending to equal net saving ($I = S$), general government purchases to equal the income from taxation ($G = NT$) and exports to equal imports ($X = M$). The equilibrium condition is that the *sum* of the three injections ($I + G + X$) equals the *sum* of our three withdrawals ($S + NT + M$).

Key definition

Equilibrium level of national income

The level of national income matched by an equivalent expenditure on domestically produced goods and services. It is also the level of national income at which the sum of injections into the inner flow is matched by the sum of withdrawals from the inner flow.

A simple Keynesian model

The circular flow model enables us to identify the incomes that flow between the principal economic agents. We can also identify the conditions for equilibrium. We now consider two important issues. First, what determines the demands for goods and services? Second, what determines the magnitude of change in the equilibrium level of national income following a change in aggregate demand?

Building a Keynesian model

The model we are building is known as a Keynesian model because it is based around ideas developed by John Maynard Keynes in the 1930s. At the heart of our Keynesian model is the idea that the level of aggregate demand 'drives' output. It is therefore important to analyse the *determinants* of aggregate demand. To do so we briefly consider the possible determinants of consumption, the injections into the circular flow and the withdrawals from the circular flow. In doing so, we outline the assumptions made in the Keynesian model about their determination. Throughout our analysis we will assume that prices are constant.

Consumption

The most significant component of aggregate demand in monetary terms is household spending. In the UK, the total value of household spending is equivalent to almost two-thirds of GDP.

The aggregate level of spending by households in the Keynesian model is assumed to be positively related to national income.

The proportion of an increase in national income spent by households is known as the **marginal propensity to consume (*mpc*)**. Therefore, if spending increases by 80p in response to an increase in national income of £1, the marginal propensity to consume out of national income is 0.8.

In reality there are other variables that also affect the aggregate level of spending. These include:

- Expected future incomes.
- The availability of credit from financial institutions.
- Interest rates and their impact on the costs to households in servicing their debts.
- The stock of debt that households have accumulated.
- Changes in the worth of financial assets (savings).
- Changes in the worth of physical assets (largely residential housing).
- Confidence (sometimes referred to as sentiment).

The level of consumption determined by factors independent of the current level of national income is known as **autonomous consumption**. These factors affect the level of spending associated with any given level of national income. So, for example, if households feel more pessimistic, they might reduce the level of spending out of their current levels of income.

Key definitions

Marginal propensity to consume (*mpc*)
The proportion of an increase in national income spent by households.

Autonomous consumption
The level of consumption that does not depend on income.

Net saving (S)

The flip side of consumption is net saving. Being the counterpart to consumption, it must be affected by national income and the list of variables identified above.

The counterpart to the marginal propensity to consume is the **marginal propensity to save (*mps*)**. The *mps* measures the proportion of an increase in national income saved by households. Because households must either save or spend their income, the sum of the *mps* and the *mpc* equals 1.

Key definition

Marginal propensity to save (*mps*)

The proportion of an increase in national income saved by households.

Net taxes (NT)

As national income rises, the amount paid in tax increases. In our presentation of the circular flow of income model we abstracted from the complexities of the tax and welfare system by assuming that the government's net taxation is collected from households. Households consume out of their **disposable income** and so taxation reduces the amount that households have to spend, while benefits increase it. Disposable income is national income (Y) less net taxation (NT).

In our simple Keynesian model, we assume that net taxation (NT) is a given proportion of factor incomes (Y). The **marginal propensity to tax (*mpt*)** is the proportion of an increase in national income paid in tax net of benefits.

The *mpt* records the proportion of a rise in national income going in taxes and in reduced benefits. For instance, if for each additional £1 of national income the tax collected from households is 20p while their benefit payments are reduced by 5p, the marginal rate of tax is 0.25.

Key definitions

Disposable income

Household income after the deduction of taxes and the addition of benefits.

Marginal propensity to tax (*mpt*)

The proportion of an increase in national income taken in tax (net of benefits).

Examples & evidence

Consumer Spending and Financial Institutions

Household consumption makes up about two-thirds of aggregate demand in the UK. Understanding its determinants is therefore important in understanding changes to national income. The obvious starting point is disposable income. Over the long term, evidence does indeed show that, after stripping out the effects of rising prices (inflation), disposable income and consumer spending grow at very, very similar rates: about 2½ per cent per annum over the past 50 years or so.

However, the statistical relationship between disposable income and consumption is different in the short term. We can see this in the chart tracking quarter-to-quarter changes in real household spending and real disposable income (%) (opposite). In other words, the chart tracks the real growth in spending and income over three-month periods.

The chart shows that quarterly consumption growth rates are typically less variable than those in disposable income. From this, economists infer that households 'smooth their spending' despite facing volatile incomes. This is known as consumption smoothing.

Consumption smoothing is facilitated by the financial system, enabling us either to borrow to supplement spending or to save to enjoy more spending in the future. Therefore, the financial system can help households to avoid large variations in their spending from, say, month to month. It

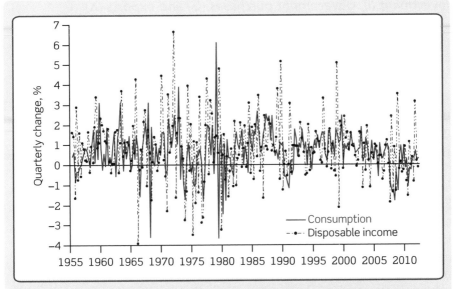

Real quarterly growth in household spending and disposable income (%).

Source: Based on data from *Quarterly National Accounts*, National Statistics (Series ABJR, HAYO and NRJR).

also means that our current spending levels are made less dependent on our current income levels. However, limitations in the availability of credit, such as those following the financial crisis of the late 2000s, impede households from smoothing their spending. This makes consumption more sensitive to current income levels.

We can expect the age of a consumer to affect the likelihood of them being a borrower or saver. Younger consumers, such as students, are more likely to be borrowing. In contrast, middle-aged consumers might be trying to save for the future by reducing their current consumption. This again points to consumers' current spending levels being affected not only by current income but also by their expected future earnings. This is something that most students can appreciate because during their time at university they will often be tapping into, as yet, unearned income!

Questions

1. How do financial institutions potentially affect the relationship between current levels of consumer spending and disposable income?
2. Under what conditions might the household sector's spending be more or less dependent on its current level of disposable income?

Investment (I), government purchases (G) and exports (X)

In the Keynesian model, we assume that investment (*I*), government purchases (*G*) and exports (*X*) are all determined independently of the country's national income. In other words, they are determined exogenously by other variables 'outside' of the model. As we shall see, this is not unreasonable, at least in the short term.

Data on investment expenditure (*I*) show that it is highly volatile. The rate of growth varies significantly from one period to another. One reason for this is that investment often involves large financial outlays. Therefore, we might identify expectations concerning *future* levels of national income, the access to finance and the cost of borrowing as variables that affect investment expenditure.

In the short term, governments typically set a budget or fiscal plan determining their spending plans for the year ahead. Therefore, it not unreasonable to assume that in the short term, government purchases are determined independently of national income. However, in the longer term, levels of government spending are likely to be more closely tied to national income since the growth of national income generates additional tax revenues with which to fund additional government spending.

Exports reflect decisions made by economic agents overseas. Therefore, in the short term, the volume of exports is likely to be determined by economic factors overseas, including overseas levels of national incomes, and by exchange rates.

Imports (M)

A proportion of household spending, of investment and of government purchases is on goods and services from overseas. We would expect the amount spent on imports to rise as incomes rise. Therefore, in the Keynesian model, it is assumed that import expenditures (*M*) are positively related to national income. The **marginal propensity to import (*mpm*)** measures the proportion of an increase in national income that is spent on imports.

Other factors, too, will affect the consumption of imports. These will affect the level of imports at any given level of national income. One factor will be the prices of imported goods and these will be affected by exchange rates. We will look at the determination of exchange rates later (see Chapter 7).

Key definition

Marginal propensity to import (*mpm*)

The proportion of an increase in national income spent on imports.

Assessment advice

Do not be confused by notation! Some of the spending by firms and government includes spending on imports. This, of course, is also true of households. It is customary to denote consumption by households on domestically produced goods and services as C_d. We could also add the subscript 'd' to investment and government purchases to denote the consumption of domestically produced goods and services. However, this is not typically done.

Recap

In the simple Keynesian model, consumption, net saving and imports are assumed to be positively related to national income. Government taxation (net of benefits) is simplified and assumed to be a constant proportion of national income. Taxation causes disposable income to be lower than national income. Investment, government purchases and exports are assumed to be exogenously determined, which means that they are determined independently of national income.

Test yourself

Q1. Explain what is meant by the concept of a marginal propensity, such as the marginal propensity to consume or the marginal propensity to import.

Q2. What does it mean when we refer to investment, government purchases and exports as being exogenously determined?

The marginal propensity to withdrawal

In focusing on the determination of national income we are concerned with the total spending on domestically produced goods and services.

The **marginal propensity to consume domestically produced goods and services (mpc_d)** measures the proportion of an increase in national income spent on domestically produced goods and services.

The counterpart to the marginal propensity to consume domestically produced goods and services is known as **the marginal propensity to withdrawal (*mpw*)**. It measures the proportion of any increase in national income that is withdrawn from the inner flow between domestic households and firms.

The marginal propensity to withdrawal is equal to the sum of the marginal propensity to save *plus* the marginal propensity to tax *plus* the marginal propensity to import. In other words, $mpw = mps + mpt + mpm$.

The sum of mpw and mpc_d must equal 1. This is because additional national income is either spent on domestically produced goods and services or withdrawn from the inner flow in the form of net saving, net taxation or imports.

Key definitions

Marginal propensity to consume domestically produced goods and services (mpc_d)

The proportion of an increase in national income that is spent on domestically produced goods and services.

Marginal propensity to withdrawal (mpw)

The proportion of an increase in national income that flows outside of the inner flow between households and firms.

Changes in aggregate demand and their impact on national income

The concept of the marginal propensity to withdraw (mpw) turns out to be crucial in determining the size of increase (decrease) in national income following a rise (fall) in aggregate demand. To illustrate, consider an increase in aggregate demand arising from an increase in injections (J) or a reduction in withdrawals (W).

In the simple Keynesian model of the economy, a rise in aggregate demand causes firms to increase output. As firms employ more resources, the flow of factor payments to households rises. This increase in income then leads to a further rise in the expenditure on firms' goods and services, a further increase in output, a further increase in income, and so on. There is a snowball effect.

However, the key point here is that each time national income rises, not all of it remains in the inner flow. Rather, some escapes in the form of withdrawals, that is as net saving (S), net taxes (NT) or imports (M). This happens because the withdrawals are positively related to national income. Equilibrium is restored when national income increases sufficiently that withdrawals rise to match the now higher level of injections.

The larger (smaller) the marginal propensity to withdrawal, the smaller (larger) the increase in national income following a rise in aggregate demand. Conversely, the larger (smaller) the marginal propensity to consume domestically produced goods and services, the larger (smaller) the increase in national income following a rise in aggregate demand.

The multiplier

We have just seen how a snowball effect arises from a change in aggregate demand. The result is that the eventual change in the size of the economy is greater than the change in aggregate demand. It is an example of what is known as **cumulative causation**: a change leads to further changes, which then snowball.

The multiplier measures the number of times larger the change in national income is compared with the initial change in aggregate demand that caused it. Therefore, we can use the multiplier to think about the change in national income that might follow a change in injections (*I*, *G* or *X*) or a change in withdrawals (*S*, *NT* and *M*). The problem for both economists and policy-makers is that in reality the chain of events that follow from some changes is often unpredictable!

The Keynesian model predicts that the size of the multiplier is dependent on the marginal propensity to withdrawal (*mpw*). The lower the *mpw*, the smaller the proportion of a change in national income that leaves the inner flow, the larger the multiplier. Conversely, the higher the *mpw*, the more of any change in national income that leaves the inner flow, thereby reducing the multiplier.

The Keynesian model predicts that the effect of a change in aggregate demand on national income will be greater, the larger the multiplier. The multiplier is inversely related to the marginal propensity to withdraw. Since the *mpw* is made up of three individual marginal propensities, the Keynesian model predicts that the effect on national income of a change in aggregate demand will be larger, the smaller the marginal propensity to save (*mps*), the smaller the marginal propensity to tax (*mpt*) and the smaller the marginal propensity to consume imports (*mpm*).

Key definitions

Cumulative causation
The name given to a chain of events that follow from an event, such as a change in government expenditure or taxation.

The multiplier
The number of times greater the change in national income is compared with the initial change in aggregate demand that caused it.

Recap

A given size of change in aggregate demand causes a snowball effect that results in a larger change in national income. This is an example of cumulative causation. The size of the multiplier is inversely related to the marginal propensity to withdrawal (*mpw*).

Test yourself

Q1. Explain the concept of the marginal propensity to withdrawal.

Q2. Explain how the multiplier works following a decrease in injections.

Alternative presentations of the Keynesian model

We now show two alternative ways of presenting the key ideas of the simple Keynesian model. Each allows us to show more formally the concepts of the equilibrium level of income, the change in the equilibrium level of national income following a change in aggregate demand and, hence, the multiplier. In other words, they allow us to analyse the Keynesian model in a little more depth.

Assessment advice

Tutors often expect students to recognise that there are two ways of solving for the equilibrium level of national income in the Keynesian model of the economy: the *income equals expenditure approach* and the *injections equals withdrawals approach*. You may be asked to do so diagrammatically or mathematically, perhaps even both. It is important that you know what approach is expected of you.

Before setting out these alternative presentational approaches of the Keynesian model, we briefly restate our simplifying assumptions about the determinants of aggregate demand that we discussed earlier:

- Consumption is positively related to national income and, after adjusting for net taxation, positively related to disposable income.
- The net tax (NT) payable by households to governments is a constant proportion of national income. Disposable income is national income *less* net taxation.
- Import expenditure (M) is positively related to national income.
- Investment (I), government expenditure (G) and exports (X) are all assumed to be determined independently of the country's national income. Consequently, they are exogenous variables.

Withdrawals–injections approach

We begin with the first of the two alternative diagrammatic presentations: the withdrawals–injection approach. Equilibrium national income occurs where withdrawals (W) equal injections (J).

The three withdrawals, namely net saving (S), net taxation (NT) and imports (M), are all positively related to national income. The marginal propensities to save, tax and import out of national income determine how much each withdrawal changes in response to a change in national income. The three marginal propensities collectively equal the marginal propensity to withdrawal out of national income.

The W-line in Figure 2.4 is the *withdrawals function*. Its slope is determined by the marginal propensity to withdrawal (mpw) out of national income.

The three injections, namely investment (I), government purchases (G) and exports (X), are exogenously determined. The J-line in Figure 2.4 is the *injections function*. Since the injections are determined independently of national income the J-line is horizontal.

> ### ✳ Assessment advice
>
> Think about the economics behind your diagrams. The J-line in Figure 2.4 is horizontal because our three injections are determined independently of national income. The W-line is drawn as linear, though this need not be the case. A linear W-line means that the marginal propensity to withdrawal is constant. If the marginal propensity to withdrawal was to rise with national income (perhaps because the marginal propensity to save was thought to increase with income), the W-line would become steeper.

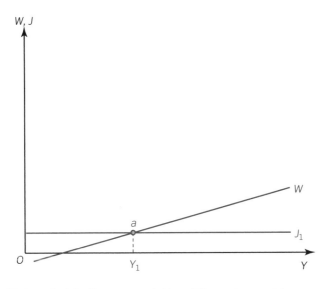

Figure 2.4 Withdrawals–injections presentation of Keynesian model.

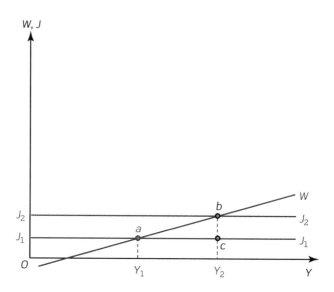

Figure 2.5 An increase in injections using the withdrawals–injections approach.

Where the W-line and J-line intersect we obtain the equilibrium national income (Y_1). Consider now an increase in injections, for instance an increase in investment. This moves the J-function up vertically from J_1 to J_2 (Figure 2.5), which is equivalent to the vertical distance $(b - c)$. The new equilibrium national income is Y_2. The increase in national income is $(Y_2 - Y_1)$ and this is equivalent to the horizontal distance $(c - a)$. The multiplier is therefore $(c - a)/(b - c)$.

The multiplier can be seen to be dependent on the slope of the withdrawals function. If we had drawn a flatter withdrawals function through point a, then the increase in national income following the rise in injections from J_1 to J_2 would have been larger. This is because a flatter withdrawals function reflects a lower marginal propensity to withdraw. The multiplier is negatively related to the marginal propensity to withdraw.

We could also use the framework to analyse the effect of a change in withdrawals. For instance, if at each level of national income withdrawals fell, perhaps because people felt more confident and so saved less of their income, the W-line would move vertically downwards. We would again find that the impact on national income is negatively related to the marginal propensity to withdrawal.

Keynesian cross

An alternative way of presenting the equilibrium national income is to identify when national income (total factor payments to households) equals aggregate demand. This can be shown diagrammatically in what is known as the Keynesian cross.

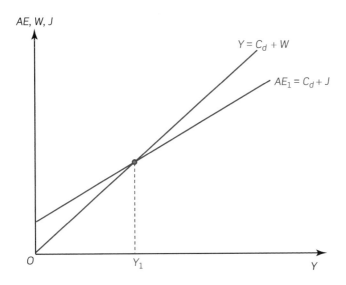

Figure 2.6 Income–expenditure presentation of Keynesian model.

National income can either be spent on domestically produced goods and services (C_d) or be a withdrawal (W) from the circular flow, that is as net saving (S), net taxation (NT) and imports (M). Therefore, if we plot $C_d + W$ against national income it must form a 45° line as in Figure 2.6.

Aggregate demand (or aggregate expenditure) is the sum of consumption on domestically produced goods and services (C_d) and injections (J). The injections take the form of investment (I), government purchases (G) and exports (X). The aggregate expenditure (AE) line plots $C_d + J$ against national income.

The consumption of domestically produced goods and services (C_d) is positively related to national income. The proportion of a change in national income spent on domestically produced goods and services is the marginal propensity to consume domestically produced goods and services. Since the three injections are determined exogenously, the slope of the AE-line is determined solely by the marginal propensity to consume domestically produced goods and services. The three injections simply move the AE-line vertically up or down. The marginal propensity is assumed to be less than 1 and so the slope of the AE-line must be flatter than our 45° line. This is illustrated by AE_1 in Figure 2.6.

The equilibrium level of national income is Y_1 where the AE-line intersects the Y-line (45° line). Consider now an increase in injections, for instance an increase in investment. This moves the AE-line vertically upwards from AE_1 to AE_2 by the distance ($b - a$) (Figure 2.7). National income rises from Y_1 to Y_2 which is mirrored in the 45° line by the vertical distance ($c - a$). The multiplier is therefore ($c - a$)/($b - a$).

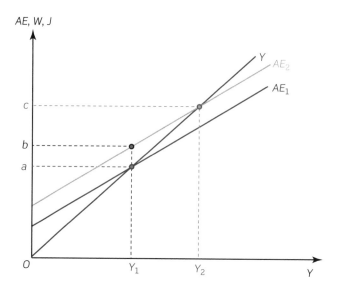

Figure 2.7 An increase in injections using the income–expenditure approach.

The size of the multiplier depends on the slope of the AE-line. If we had drawn a flatter AE-line intersecting the 45° line at Y_1 before then increasing injections, we would have found the new equilibrium level of national income to be at an income level below Y_2. This is because the slope of the AE-line is the marginal propensity to consume domestically produced goods and services. A flatter AE-line is caused by a lower marginal propensity to consume domestically produced goods and services. Since the marginal propensity to withdraw and the marginal propensity to consume domestically produced goods and services must equal 1, the multiplier is smaller when the marginal propensity to consume domestically produced goods is smaller.

Recap

We can analyse the impact of a change in aggregate demand on national income in a simple Keynesian model using one of two approaches: a withdrawals–injections approach or an income–expenditure approach. Both approaches can be presented diagrammatically.

Test yourself

Q1. Using the income–expenditure approach, construct a diagram to show the effect on national income of a fall in injections.

Q2. Using the withdrawals–injections approach, construct a diagram to show the effect on national income of an increase in withdrawals.

Limitations of the Keynesian model

The simple Keynesian model is a demand-driven model of the economy: changes in aggregate demand lead to multiplied effects on national income. The model assumes that firms respond to changes in the demand for their goods and services by adjusting their output accordingly. This means that supply decisions are entirely dependent on demand. This is a keenly debated issue among economists. Some economists go so far as to argue that supply decisions are made independently of demand! In essence, this is a debate about the economy's aggregate supply function.

The Keynesian model assumes that firms are able and willing to adjust supply to changes in demand. But how reasonable is this assumption? As firms change their level of output, they too are adjusting the volume of inputs used in production, including, of course, their employment of labour. This has implications for costs. A key question is what happens to firms' average costs as they change their levels of output. A firm's average cost is calculated as its total cost divided by its level of output. In other words, it is the cost per unit of output (unit cost). If in raising output levels to meet increased demand firms find that their unit costs rise, they will look to raise the prices paid by customers. However, this will choke off some of the increase in aggregate demand.

The impact of changes in aggregate demand on firms' costs is likely to depend, at least in part, on current levels of production. Therefore, the conclusions of the circular flow of income model in respect of aggregate demand changes on national income are likely to be more valid, the more spare capacity firms have. On the other hand, when there is less spare capacity in the economy, the less the national income is likely to increase following a rise in aggregate demand and the more prices will rise.

Recap

The simple Keynesian model assumes that prices are constant and that firms' output decisions are dependent on the current level of aggregate demand.

Test yourself

Draw up a list of reasons why firms might *not* increase their output (or increase output very little) despite an increase in the current level of demand for their goods and services.

Chapter summary – pulling it all together

By the end of this chapter you should be able to:

	Confident ✓	Not confident?
Identify the principal economic agents in the economy		Revise pages 31–36
Identify the income flows between the principal economic agents in the economy		Revise pages 31–36
Identify the injections into the circular flow of income and describe their impact on aggregate demand		Revise pages 32–36
Identify the withdrawals from the circular flow of income and describe their impact on aggregate demand		Revise pages 32–36
Use a diagram to represent the circular flow of income model of the economy		Revise pages 31–37
Explain what is meant by the equilibrium level of national income in the circular flow model		Revise page 37
Analyse the simplifying assumptions made about the components of aggregate demand when constructing the simple Keynesian model		Revise pages 38–43
Explain the concepts of cumulative causation and the multiplier and the factors affecting the size of the multiplier		Revise pages 44–45
Illustrate diagrammatically the effect of a change in aggregate demand on national income using the injections–withdrawal and/or the income–expenditure approach		Revise pages 46–50
Analyse some of the possible limitations of the simple Keynesian model		Revise page 51

Now try the assessment question at the start of this chapter, using the answer guidelines below.

Answer guidelines

* Assessment question

With the aid of a diagram, describe the income flows in the circular flow of income model. Using a simple Keynesian model, discuss the impact on national income of a *reduction* in injections into the circular flow.

Approaching the question

The question provides an opportunity for you to demonstrate your understanding of the circular flow and simple Keynesian models. In doing so, you can show your awareness of the principal economic agents in the economy, the flows of income that connect them and how these flows of income help determine the level of aggregate demand. You can then develop these ideas to consider how changes in aggregate demand might influence the level of national income.

Important points to include

- **The circular flow of income diagram.** Using a circular flow of income diagram, identify the principal economic actors in the economy and the flows of income that connect them. Introduce the concepts of injections, withdrawals and aggregate demand.

- **Injections, aggregate demand and the circular flow.** Explain how a reduction in injections would, all other things remaining equal, reduce aggregate demand. In response to the reduction in aggregate demand, firms reduce their output. The equilibrium level of national income will fall.

- **Constructing the simple Keynesian model.** To explore the extent to which a reduction in injections might affect national income, construct the simple Keynesian model. You can use either the income–expenditure or the injections–withdrawals approach depending on what it is expected of you.

- **The magnitude of impact on national income.** Applying the simple Keynesian framework, explore how a change in aggregate demand has a multiplied effect on the equilibrium level of national income. In doing so, apply the concepts of the multiplier, cumulative causation and the marginal propensity to withdrawal.

Make your answer stand out

- The depth of your analysis is important. Try to demonstrate a mastery of economic concepts and ideas. Wherever possible, draw on real-world examples and instigate a discussion.

- In constructing your diagrams, ensure that your supporting text clearly explains the underlying economic concepts and ideas. This will help to provide a depth to your analysis.

- Enter into a discussion concerning the factors that might affect the change in national income following the reduction in injections. You can discuss the merits and drawbacks of the simple Keynesian model.

Read to impress

Here are some books, articles and other sources that you can use to develop your answers on the topic area.

Books

Griffiths, A. and Wall, S. (2011) *Economics for Business and Management*, 3rd edition, Chapter 9, 'National income determination'. Harlow, UK: Pearson Education

Parkin, M., Powell, M. and Matthews, K. (2012) *Essential Economics*, European edition, Chapter 10, 'Real GDP'. Harlow, UK: Pearson Education

Sloman, J. and Garratt, D. (2013) *Essentials of Economics*, 6th edition, Chapter 8, 'Aggregate demand and the national economy'. Harlow, UK: Pearson Education.

Articles

Berry, S. and Williams, R. (2009) Household saving. *Bank of England Quarterly Bulletin*, Q3: 191–201 (www.bankofengland.co.uk/publications/quarterlybulletin/qb090302.pdf).

Bunn, P., Le Roux, J., Johnson, R. and McLeay, M. (2012) Influences on household spending: evidence from the 2012 NMG Consulting survey. *Bank of England Quarterly Bulletin*, Q4: 332–42 (www.bankofengland.co.uk/publications/Documents/quarterlybulletin/qb120403.pdf).

Nielsen, M., Pezzini, S., Reinold, K. and Williams, R. (2010) The financial position of British households: evidence from the 2010 NMG Consulting survey. *Bank of England Quarterly Bulletin*, Q4: 333–45 (www.bankofengland.co.uk/publications/quarterlybulletin/qb100408.pdf).

Periodicals and newspapers

The Bank of England's *Inflation Report* contains a readable overview of recent patterns in the component expenditures of UK aggregate demand.

The *Office for National Statistics* publishes a range of relevant data and supporting commentaries on the economy. These include releases relating to national income, expenditure and output. Information relating to these topic areas can be accessed at: www.ons.gov.uk/ons/taxonomy/index.html?nscl=National+Income%2C+Expenditure+and+Output

Financial Times (2011) Now is the time to eat, drink and be merry. Samuel Brittan, 29 December.

Financial Times (2012) Today's challenges go beyond Keynes. Jeffrey Sachs, 17 December.

Financial Times (2012) Spending reigned in as debt fears bite. Claire Jones, 18 December.

New York Times (2011) Keynes was right. Paul Krugman, 29 December.

Companion website

Go to the companion website at **www.pearsoned.co.uk/econexpress** to find more revision support online for this topic area.

Notes

3

The *AD–AS* model

Topic map

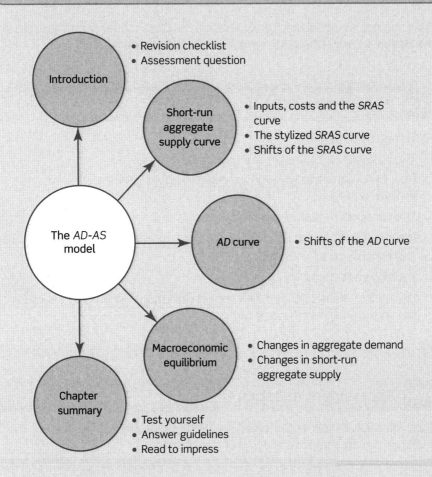

- Revision checklist
- Assessment question

Introduction

Short-run aggregate supply curve
- Inputs, costs and the *SRAS* curve
- The stylized *SRAS* curve
- Shifts of the *SRAS* curve

The *AD-AS* model

AD curve
- Shifts of the *AD* curve

Macroeconomic equilibrium
- Changes in aggregate demand
- Changes in short-run aggregate supply

Chapter summary
- Test yourself
- Answer guidelines
- Read to impress

A printable version of this topic map is available from **www.pearsoned.co.uk/econexpress**

Introduction

When we analysed a simple Keynesian model of the economy (Chapter 2), we used it to consider how changes to aggregate demand (the total demand for firms' goods and services) affect the size of the economy. The model is a demand-driven model of the economy. This means that it is the level of aggregate demand that determines the size of the economy. However, this ignores other variables that could potentially affect firms' output decisions, such as input costs, technological constraints and the degree of spare capacity.

The *AD–AS* model of the economy allows us to consider how the *interaction* of aggregate demand (*AD*) and aggregate supply (*AS*) determines both the size of the economy and the average price of domestically produced goods and services.

In this chapter we show how to construct the *AD–AS* model before considering how changes in *AD* and/or *AS may* affect output and prices.

 Revision checklist

What you need to know:
- ❏ The possible limitations of the circular flow model.
- ❏ How to construct a short-run aggregate supply (*SRAS*) curve and explain its *slope*.
- ❏ The variables that *shift* the *SRAS* curve.
- ❏ How to construct the *AD* curve and explain its *slope*.
- ❏ The variables that *shift* the *AD* curve.
- ❏ Equilibrium in the *AD–AS* model.
- ❏ Changes in *AD* and *AS* and their impact on national income and prices in the short run and in the long run.

 Assessment question

Can you answer this essay-type question? Guidelines on answering the question are presented at the end of this chapter.

Using the *AD–AS* framework, consider the effects of an *increase* in government expenditure on output and prices.

Short-run aggregate supply

The simple Keynesian model assumes that firms adjust their output deci-sions in response to demand changes. Consequently, it does not consider the extent to which firms are actually both able and willing to adjust their output. Changes to output require adjustments in the use of resources. This is why economists look to model the economy's supply curve. We begin by consider-ing this curve in the short run.

Our aim is to plot for the economy an **aggregate supply** (*AS*) curve. This is a curve showing the total amount that firms in the economy are willing to supply at each level of prices. Since this is a supply curve for the economy and not for a single firm or market, output corresponds to the range of final goods and services provided by the country's *domestic* producers. Therefore, the economy's price level is an *average* price level across the range of final goods and services. The average price level for the economy is referred to as the **GDP deflator** (see Chapter 1).

Key definitions

Aggregate supply
The total volume of domestically produced goods and services.

GDP deflator
The name given to the average price level of domestically produced goods and services.

Recap

The aggregate supply curve shows the total amount of goods and services that domestic producers are willing to supply at each level of economy-wide prices.

Test yourself

Q1. How is the aggregate supply curve different from that for an individual firm?

Q2. What is the price level against which the aggregate supply curve is drawn?

Inputs, costs and the *SRAS* curve

A key consideration is the shape of the economy's short-run aggregate supply curve. This is dependent on the extent to which firms' costs change as they adjust their output levels. A simplifying assumption is to assume that in the short run the 'menu' of prices paid by firms for their inputs is fixed. In drawing the short-run aggregate supply curve we are therefore assuming a given set of input prices. In effect, we are assuming that input prices exhibit 'stickiness' in the short run. This is not entirely unreasonable, especially in the case of labour where wage rates are typically set for one or two years.

Intuitively, we might expect more domestically produced goods and services to be provided the higher the economy's average price level. This implies that the aggregate supply curve slopes upwards. But can we be more specific about the extent to which it *may* slope upwards?

At this point we need to consider the technical relationship between inputs and output, that is the adjustment firms need to make in their use of resources to bring about a given change in the volume of output. This relationship is known as a **production function**. In effect, this captures prevailing technologies and ways of doing things. In the short run we shall assume that these are fixed. Firms' production functions help to determine their costs in adjusting output. Consequently, they determine the shape of the aggregate supply curve too.

In the short run, firms looking to change their volume of output are constrained by the resources they can adjust. This reflects current technological know-how and the likelihood that some resources can be adjusted very little, if at all, in the short run. It is customary to model non-financial fixed assets used in production, such as the amount of office or factory space, as being 'fixed' in the short run. These inputs are known more simply as **physical capital**. Therefore, to adjust their volume of output, firms must, in the short run, adjust the levels of those inputs that are 'variable'. These inputs include labour, raw materials and consumables ('day-to-day' inputs).

Key definitions

Production function

A function that describes the relationship between inputs and output. A production function can be for either an individual firm or an economy as a whole.

Physical capital (non-financial fixed assets)

Inputs that can be used for a protracted period of time, usually more than one year, in the production of goods and services.

Now assume that firms are looking to increase the quantity of variable inputs so that they can raise output. The volume of additional resources needed may depend on existing levels of output. In the presence of fixed quantities of capital, firms are likely to reach a level of output when to keep raising output by a given amount will require increasingly larger amounts of additional variable inputs. This is the idea that variable inputs exhibit diminishing marginal returns. The important point here is that this has implications for the cost of increasing output: the additional cost of increasing output rises as output rises. Consequently, the average cost of production will rise too.

Therefore, the assumption of a fixed stock of capital in the economy helps to explain why the *SRAS* curve is typically drawn as becoming steeper as output rises. This effect is likely to be reinforced by the growing scarcity of variable inputs, like labour, at higher and higher levels of output. Workers, for instance, are typically paid higher rates for working overtime. Again, the result is that marginal costs will rise as output increases.

Key definition

Diminishing marginal returns

The decline in the additional amount of output that results from increasing an input while the quantity of other inputs remains constant.

Stylised *SRAS* curve

A stylised (or hypothetical) version of the *SRAS* curve is shown in Figure 3.1. At low levels of output up to Y_1, the curve shows that firms in aggregate are willing to increase output without an increase in output prices. This is consistent with the circular flow of income model. However, beyond Y_1 larger and larger increases in prices are needed to induce additional output. At Y_f, firms are unable to increase output further. This maximum level of output should not be confused with the economy's **potential output**. The economy's potential output occurs when its inputs are being employed at normal levels of utilisation. Therefore, it is the economy's sustainable output level. As output expands up to Y_f, inputs are being used increasingly intensively and a point is reached when firms are operating at above normal capacity. There is, of course, a limit to this and this is what Y_f shows. Potential output is therefore *below* Y_f.

Key definition

Potential output

The economy's output level when resources are being employed at normal levels of utilisation and which is sustainable over the longer term.

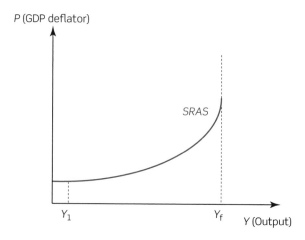

P (GDP deflator)

SRAS

Y_1

Y_f

Y (Output)

Figure 3.1 Stylised short-run aggregate supply curve.

❋ Assessment advice

Take care with terminology. The economy's potential output is not the same as its full-capacity output. It is the economy's sustainable output level. The economy's output can exceed its potential output.

Examples & evidence

Output gaps

When the economy's *actual* output diverges from its *potential* output, the economy experiences an output gap. It is important to recognise that potential output is that level of output when the economy's resources, such as its workforce or firms' plant and equipment, are being used at normal levels of intensity. It is also known as the economy's 'sustainable' or 'natural' level of output. Full-capacity output is higher, but it, too, is constrained by the availability of resources and the extent to which these resources can be used ever more intensively.

A negative output gap occurs when the economy's output is *below* the economy's potential output. Negative output gaps tend to occur when economic growth is weak or even negative. A positive output gap occurs when the economy's output is *above* its potential output. Positive output gaps tend to occur during periods of strong economic growth (see Chapter 4).

While actual output is observable, potential output is estimated. Estimates can be generated by analysing the responses to surveys of business.

Potential output can also be estimated by using statistical techniques. There are two general statistical approaches. First, a trend growth path can be 'fitted' through actual output (real GDP) data. Second, a model of the economy's production function can be built. The model enables modellers to estimate the effectiveness of the economy's resources and therefore the level of output if these resources are being used at normal levels of intensity. Official estimates of the economy's output gaps, such as those issued by the European Union or the Organization for Economic Cooperation and Development (OECD), tend to use this production function approach.

The chart below shows the UK's output gap since 1965. The figures are expressed as a percentage of the economy's estimated potential output. The period between 2008 and 2013 is especially noteworthy, with the economy's output typically 3½ per cent below its potential.

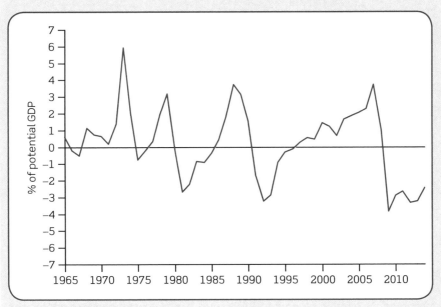

UK output gap, 1965–2014.

Note: 2012 to 2014 are forecasts.
Source: Based on data from AMECO database (European Commission, DGECFIN), Table 6.5. http://ec.europAa.eu/economy_finance/ameco/user/serie/SelectSerie.cfm.

Questions

1. Explain how actual output can exceed potential output.

2. Why might we expect price pressures to emerge if the economy is operating above its potential output level?

Assessment advice

Perhaps the way that your tutor has drawn the *SRAS* curve looks slightly different. This reflects differences among economists about the *precise* nature of this relationship. The mainstream view is that the *SRAS* curve becomes steeper as the level of output rises. The important point here is to understand the theoretical foundations in the construction of the curve.

Recap

The *SRAS* curve plots the aggregate amount of output that firms are willing and able to supply at different values of the GDP deflator. In constructing the curve, we assume a given level of technological know-how, a given stock of capital and that input prices are constant. The mainstream view is that the *SRAS* curve grows increasingly steeper as the economy's output level rises.

Test yourself

Q1. Explain the mainstream view as to why the *SRAS* becomes progressively steeper.

Q2. What sorts of items are included within the economy's stock of capital?

Shifts of the *SRAS* curve

The *SRAS* curve shows the impact of a change in output prices on the volume of output in the economy. The effect of a change in the GDP deflator on output represents a move *along* an *SRAS* curve. But there are other variables that affect the level of output (real GDP). Changes in these will lead to a *shift* of the *SRAS* curve.

In constructing the *SRAS* curve we hold certain variables constant. If these change then we have a new *SRAS* curve. Among these are input prices. Changes in wage rates or the price of raw materials affect firms' costs. This, in turn, affects the amount of goods and services that firms are willing to supply at each price level. A decrease in input costs will increase the amount that firms are willing to supply at each price level. This is consistent with a downward shift of the *SRAS* curve, such as that from $SRAS_1$ to $SRAS_2$ as shown in Figure 3.2. It is assumed that the economy's full capacity output, Y_f, is not affected.

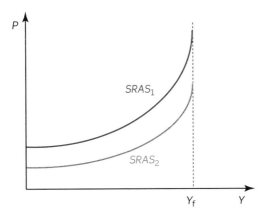

Figure 3.2 Increase in short-run aggregate supply curve (no change in full-capacity output).

We also hold the amount of physical capital constant in the short run. An increase in the amount of physical capital per worker is known as **capital deepening**. It raises the productivity of labour enabling more to be produced. Hence, an increase in physical capital is also consistent with an increase in aggregate supply. Similarly, an advancement in technology and know-how allows firms to produce more, even when other things, such as the quantity of inputs, remain constant.

Increasing amounts of capital and technological progress not only cause the *SRAS* curve to move rightwards, but also raise the economy's potential output and its full-capacity output. This is illustrated in Figure 3.3. A similar effect arises from an increase in the size of a country's labour force or an increase in a country's stock of **human capital**. Human capital is the term used to describe the skills, expertise and health of the population.

Key definitions

Capital deepening
An increase in the amount of capital per worker.

Human capital
The skills, expertise and health of the population.

In industrialised economies, we have observed over many years an accumulation of physical capital, capital deepening, technological advance and rising levels of human capital. This means that the *SRAS* curves are continually shifting rightwards in these countries. The speed of this movement is then

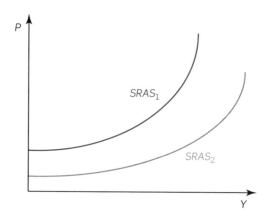

Figure 3.3 Increase in short-run aggregate supply curve with an increase in full-capacity output.

reflected in a country's long-term rate of economic growth. Those countries with the highest longer-term rates of economic growth will have seen the greatest rightward shift of the *SRAS* curve.

Recap

A change in the economy's GDP deflator results in a movement along the short-run aggregate supply (*SRAS*) curve. If any of the variables held constant when constructing the *SRAS* curve change, then the curve shifts. Some of these changes can also affect the economy's potential output. Over the longer term, the curve moves rightwards, generating long-term economic growth.

Test yourself

Q1. Show the effect on the *SRAS* curve of capital deepening.

Q2. Show the impact on the *SRAS* curve of a fall in the price of oil.

Aggregate demand curve

Aggregate demand (*AD*) is the total demand for the output of domestic producers. The *AD* curve plots the relationship between the level of aggregate demand and the economy's average price level (GDP deflator). An illustrative

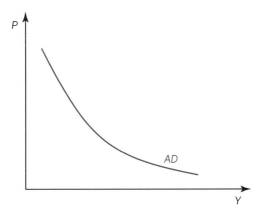

Figure 3.4 Aggregate demand curve.

AD curve is shown in Figure 3.4 where the level of aggregate demand falls as the economy's average price level rises. But why might we expect the total demand for firms' output to rise as the average price level falls?

If we think about the demand curve for an individual product, a key reason why less of the product is bought as its price rises is that people switch to alternative products. Although **substitution effects** are fairly intuitive at a microeconomic level, what are the substitutes to the economy's current output? We consider three possibilities.

First, as domestically produced goods and services become more expensive, consumers may switch to foreign alternatives. Overseas consumers, too, may switch away from goods and services originating here. The effect is that export volumes fall, import volumes rise and, therefore, aggregate demand falls.

Second, as the economy's average price level rises, consumption may switch from the present to the future. With higher prices, consumers require more money with which to make transactions. With a given stock of money (money supply), an increase in the demand for money to make transactions (transactions demand for money) will put upward pressure on interest rates. Higher interest rates motivate individuals to increase saving while also discouraging borrowing. In other words, higher interest rates result in a substitution effect with consumers postponing current consumption in favour of higher future consumption.

Third, economic agents may switch between the consumption of goods and services and the accumulation of financial assets. The latter occurs through saving. With higher prices there is an incentive for saving to increase because the real value or the purchasing power of financial assets, other things being equal, is eroded. This substitution effect is also known as a **real balance effect**.

Aggregate demand

The total level of spending on goods and services made in the economy.

Substitution effects

The incentive to switch to (or from) domestically produced goods and services when the average price level of domestically produced goods and services falls (or rises).

Real balance effect

The impact on the purchasing power of our financial assets resulting from changes in the average price level of domestically produced goods and services.

Recap

The aggregate demand curve shows the total amount of domestically produced goods and services demanded at each level of economy-wide prices. Its downward slope can be explained by a series of substitution effects that result in aggregate demand falling as prices rise.

Test yourself

Q1. How different are the concepts of an aggregate demand curve and the demand curve for an individual product?

Q2. If the GDP deflator *falls*, how can substitution effects explain the *increase* in aggregate demand?

Shifts of the *AD* curve

The *AD* curve shows how changes in the average price of domestically pro-duced goods and services affect aggregate demand. A change in the GDP deflator results in *moves* along the *AD* curve. Variables other than price that affect aggregate demand result in a *shift* of the *AD* curve. When these 'other variables' increase aggregate demand, the *AD* curve moves right-wards, but when they decrease aggregate demand, the *AD* curve moves leftwards.

Figure 3.5 illustrates that an increase in aggregate demand results in a rightward shift of the *AD* curve. At each price level, aggregate demand

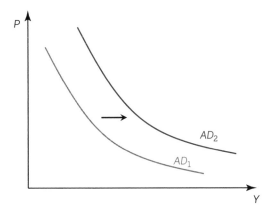

Figure 3.5 Increase in aggregate demand.

is higher. Among the factors that could cause an *increase* in aggregate demand are:

- *Reduction in interest rates.* A reduction in interest rates reduces borrowing costs. This could motivate firms to invest in new capital or households to obtain credit to fund consumption.
- *Increase in the quantity of money.* An increase in the stock of money, including the value of deposit and savings accounts that can be readily converted into cash, will encourage consumption by both households and firms.
- *Increase in government consumption.* Government spending on goods and services is a component of aggregate demand. If this increases, all other things being equal, then aggregate demand increases too.
- *Reduction in taxes or an increase in welfare payments.* A reduction in taxes or an increase in welfare payments increases the disposable income of households. In turn, this increases spending and so the level of aggregate demand.
- *Optimistic expectations.* If households expect future income growth to be strong, this will help to boost current consumption. Similarly, if firms are optimistic about future profits, they may be encouraged to invest in new physical capital. Both would increase aggregate demand.

Recap

A change in the economy's average price level (GDP deflator) results in a movement along the aggregate demand curve. Changes to aggregate demand caused by variables other than the GDP deflator result in a shift of the aggregate demand curve.

Macroeconomic equilibrium

Having constructed our *AD* and *AS* curves we are now in a position to put the two together. In doing so we can trace through the effects of *fluctuations* in aggregate demand and short-run aggregate supply on the economy's output and on prices.

Macroeconomic equilibrium in the *AD–AS* model can be found where the two curves intersect, as illustrated in Figure 3.6. This allows us to identify the price level (P_1 in Figure 3.6) at which aggregate demand equals the volume of output supplied. At prices above the equilibrium level, firms collectively are unable to sell all their output and will look to reduce prices until the excess supply is eliminated. At prices below the equilibrium level there are shortages and firms will increase prices, thereby eliminating the excess demand.

Key definition

Macroeconomic equilibrium.

The equilibrium that occurs when the total demand for domestically produced goods and services equals the total output of domestically produced goods and services.

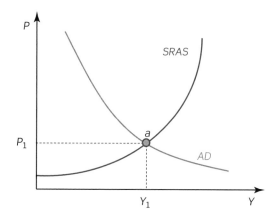

Figure 3.6 Macroeconomic equilibrium.

Changes in aggregate demand

Aggregate demand is subject to volatility. This is a theme pursued later (see Chapter 4). In the simple Keynesian model (Chapter 2), a change in aggregate demand affected only output. Prices are constant. We can employ the AD–AS model to see how changes in aggregate demand may affect both output *and* prices. To see how, consider an increase in government purchases (assume that taxes remain unchanged).

Assume that the economy is initially in equilibrium at point a, (P_1, Y_1), as shown in Figure 3.7, and assume that the economy's output Y_1 is consistent with the economy's potential output, that is its sustainable longer-term output. The increase in aggregate demand resulting from higher government spending on domestically produced goods and services causes the AD curve to shift rightwards from AD_1 to AD_2. A new equilibrium occurs at point b, (P_2, Y_2). With input prices constant in the short run, the higher GDP deflator induces firms to increase output. If the aggregate supply curve had been horizontal through point a, as in the simple Keynesian model (see Chapter 2), the increase in output would have been $Y_3 - Y_1$, equivalent to the horizontal difference $(c - a)$.

> ### ✳ Assessment advice
>
> Be aware of how the impact on national income from an increase in aggregate demand is sensitive to the assumptions we make about the economy. For instance, we can see from Figure 3.7 that the same increase in aggregate demand will have more impact on output (Y) and less impact on the GDP deflator (P), the flatter the AS curve. The increase in national income is largest when the AS curve is horizontal. In this scenario, output prices are unaffected.

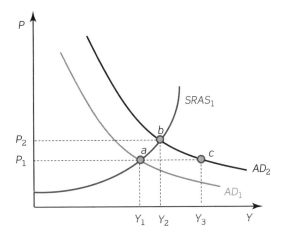

Figure 3.7 Increase in aggregate demand: short-term impact

The economy's new equilibrium output, Y_2, is now above the economy's sustainable longer-term level. In other words, assuming that the increase in aggregate demand has not impacted on the economy's potential output, there is now a positive output gap. This suggests that forces should work to eliminate this. However, economists disagree over the speed at which this will happen. Nonetheless, we can use the AD–AS model to consider how output could adjust further.

Input prices are assumed fixed in the short term. However, with the GDP deflator higher, the suppliers of inputs, including workers, will find that their incomes will purchase fewer goods and services. In response, the suppliers of inputs will look to increase prices to restore the real value of their factor payments. Workers, for instance, will look to negotiate higher nominal (actual) wages. As input prices rise, the SRAS curve shifts vertically upwards from $SRAS_1$ (Figure 3.8). This is because firms become willing to supply less at each price level. The effect of this could result in the SRAS curve moving to $SRAS_2$ and the economy returning to its potential output, Y_1, but with prices now higher at P_3. Therefore, the possible longer-term equilibrium is point c, (P_3, Y_1).

Recap

An increase (decrease) in aggregate demand will result in a short-term macroeconomic equilibrium with a higher (lower) GDP deflator and a higher (lower) level of output. In the longer term further adjustments may take place, driving the economy towards its potential output.

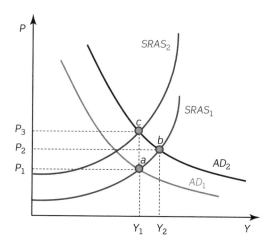

Figure 3.8 Increase in aggregate demand: longer-term impact.

Changes in short-run aggregate supply

Economic analysis tends to focus on aggregate demand as the principal driver of changes in output and prices. However, changes in *SRAS* can also drive changes in output and prices. One commonly cited example is the price of oil. We can use the *AD–AS* model to work through how an increase in the price of oil (or other inputs) might affect the economy.

Assume that the economy starts at point *a*, (P_1, Y_1), in Figure 3.9 and that Y_1 is the economy's potential output. The rise in the price of oil will cause the *SRAS* curve to shift upwards. This is because at each price level the volume of output that firms are collectively willing to supply is now lower. Assume for simplicity that the economy's potential output is not affected. The economy will move to a new equilibrium at point *b*, (P_2, Y_2), where the GDP deflator is higher, but where output is lower and now below its potential level.

With the economy's level of output below the potential level, further adjustments in the economy can be expected. One possibility is that input prices might fall. If this happened then it would begin to reverse the upward shift of the *SRAS* curve. In other words, the *SRAS* curve would shift downwards from

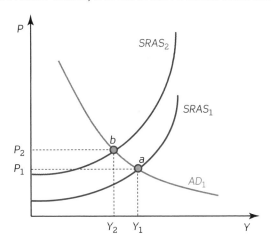

Figure 3.9 Decrease in short-run aggregate supply: short-term impact.

*SRAS*₂ perhaps to its original position with output and prices returning to their original levels. However, the speed of such an adjustment is open to question, particularly given that it requires input prices, including workers' wages, to fall.

With 'sticky' input prices, particularly in a downward direction, some economists would advocate that government should boost aggregate demand when output and employment are below their natural levels. This would involve government increasing spending and/or lowering taxes. The aim would be to move the *AD* curve to the right and so to AD_2 as shown in Figure 3.10. Macroeconomic equilibrium would be at point c, (P_3, Y_1), with output again at its potential level but with the GDP deflator higher at P_3.

Recap

A decrease (increase) in *SRAS* will result in a short-term macroeconomic equilibrium with a higher (lower) GDP deflator and a lower (higher) level of output. In the longer term, further adjustments may take place, driving the economy towards its potential output, though in the case where *SRAS* has fallen, it may be that policies to boost aggregate demand are required.

Test yourself

Q1. Use the *AD–AS* model to illustrate the short-term impact on the economy of an increase in *SRAS* from a decline in the price of oil.

Q2. Consider the longer-term impact on the economy if at the new equilibrium the economy's output deviates from the economy's potential output.

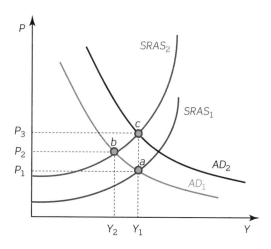

Figure 3.10 Boosting aggregate demand following a decrease in short-run aggregate supply.

Chapter summary – pulling it all together

By the end of this chapter you should be able to:

	Confident ✓	Not confident?
Analyse the potential strengths and weaknesses of the simple Keynesian model		Revise pages 58–59
Explain the theoretical foundations of the *SRAS* curve and hence its potential shape		Revise pages 59–64
Distinguish between movements along the *SRAS* curve and shifts of the *SRAS* curve		Revise pages 64–65
Illustrate through diagrams changes in *SRAS*		Revise pages 64–66
Explain the theoretical foundations of the *AD* curve and hence its potential shape		Revise pages 66–68
Distinguish between movements along the *AD* curve and shifts of the *AD* curve		Revise pages 68–69
Illustrate through diagrams changes in aggregate demand		Revise pages 68–70
Explain using *AD–AS* diagrams the concept of macroeconomic equilibrium		Revise page 70
Explain using *AD–AS* diagrams the impact on the economy of changes in aggregate demand in the short term and the possibilities in the longer term		Revise pages 71–73
Explain using *AD–AS* diagrams the impact on the economy of changes in short-run aggregate supply in the short term and the possibilities in the longer term		Revise pages 73–74

Now try the assessment question at the start of this chapter, using the answer guidelines below.

Answer guidelines

✳ Assessment question

Using the *AD–AS* framework, consider the effects of an *increase* in government expenditure on output and prices.

Approaching the question

The question provides an opportunity for you to demonstrate your understanding of the *AD–AS* model and how, in particular, it can be used to consider the impact of changes in aggregate demand (or short-run aggregate supply) on both output *and* prices. In addressing the question, you can expect to explain with the aid of diagrams the construction of the *AD* and *SRAS* curves, the interaction of *AD* and *SRAS*, and adjustments to a new macroeconomic equilibrium following changes in government spending.

Important points to include

- **Theoretical foundations of the *AD* and *AS* curves.** Some elaboration of the construction of the *AD* and *AS* curves is expected. The extent of this elaboration will, in part, depend on the precise nature of your assessment brief.

- **Macroeconomic equilibrium.** With the aid of a diagram(s), explain the meaning of equilibrium in the *AD–AS* model.

- **Adjustment to a new macroeconomic equilibrium.** With the aid of diagrams, explain the impact on the economy of a change in aggregate demand following the increase in government spending. In particular, illustrate the movement of the *AD* curve and its effect on prices and output.

Make your answer stand out

- Be sure to use diagrams and to label them correctly. Diagrams need to be fully explained and should support your written explanation.
- Better answers will consider both the short-term impact of the change in government spending on the economy and further adjustments that

may take place. The latter gives you some opportunity to develop your answer and to reflect on the differences among economists and policy-makers in their understanding of how economies work and the role that governments can play.

Read to impress

Here are some books, articles and other sources that you can use to develop your answers on the topic area.

Books

Griffiths, A. and Wall, S. (2011) *Economics for Business and Management*, 3rd edition, Chapter 9, 'National income determination'. Harlow, UK: Pearson Education.

Parkin, M., Powell, M. and Matthews, K. (2012) *Essential Economics*, European edition, Chapter 14, 'Aggregate supply and aggregate demand'. Harlow, UK: Pearson Education.

Sloman, J. and Garratt, D. (2013) *Essentials of Economics*, 6th edition, Chapter 9, 'Aggregate supply and growth'. Harlow, UK: Pearson Education.

Articles

Benito, A., Neiss, K., Price, S. and Lukasz, R. (2010) The impact of the financial crisis on supply. *Bank of England Quarterly Bulletin*, Q2: 104–14 (www.bankofengland.co.uk/publications/Documents/quarterlybulletin/qb090302.pdf).

Periodicals and newspapers

The Bank of England's *Inflation Report* contains a readable overview of recent patterns in the economy.

The *Office for National Statistics* publishes a range of relevant data and supporting commentaries on the economy. These include releases relating to national income, expenditure and output. Information relating to these topic areas can be accessed at: www.ons.gov.uk/ons/taxonomy/index.html?nscl=National+Income%2C+Expenditure+and+Output

Financial Times (2011) UK economy: in search of roots. Samuel Brittan, 20 March.

Financial Times (2012) Questions at the heart of UK economic policy. Gavyn Davies, 12 August.

Financial Times (2012) £58 billion funding plan delights regions. Andrew Bounds, John Murray Brown and Chris Tighe, 5 December.

Companion website

Go to the companion website at **www.pearsoned.co.uk/econexpress** to find more revision support online for this topic area.

Notes

4   The business cycle

Topic map

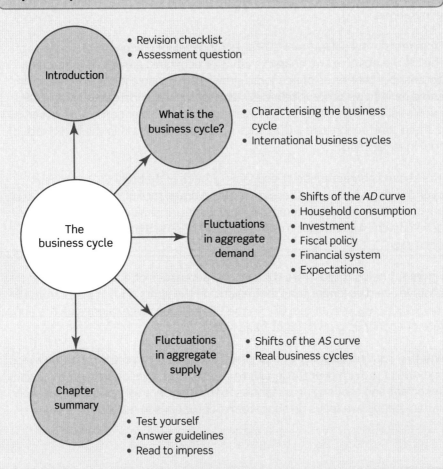

- Revision checklist
- Assessment question

Introduction

What is the business cycle?
- Characterising the business cycle
- International business cycles

The business cycle

Fluctuations in aggregate demand
- Shifts of the *AD* curve
- Household consumption
- Investment
- Fiscal policy
- Financial system
- Expectations

Fluctuations in aggregate supply
- Shifts of the *AS* curve
- Real business cycles

Chapter summary
- Test yourself
- Answer guidelines
- Read to impress

A printable version of this topic map is available from **www.pearsoned.co.uk/econexpress**

Introduction

As we saw earlier (Chapter 1), one of the most fundamental issues in macro-economics is a country's economic growth. Economic growth is measured by the growth in real GDP (output) between two moments in time. We tend to distinguish between short-term economic growth and long-term economic growth.

Short-term growth can be thought of as referring to growth between two moments in time that are in reasonably close proximity, for example growth over a 3-month or a 12-month period. It is short-term growth that we tend to hear reference to in the media, particularly when the Office for National Statistics (ONS) releases its latest briefing on the size of the economy. In contrast, long-term growth is growth over many years, perhaps many decades or generations.

From merely 'eyeballing' real GDP data for developed economies, like that of the UK, we observe two characteristics of economic growth. The first characteristic is that rates of economic growth are variable in the short term. In some periods we observe relatively large percentage increases in real GDP, such as in the late 1980s in the UK. In contrast, in other periods we observe a sharp contraction in real GDP, such as in 2009 in the UK in the aftermath of the financial crisis.

The second characteristic of economic growth is that real GDP increases over the longer term. In other words, the average rate of growth over time is positive. However, when comparing economies at similar stages of economic development we find that the average rate of growth over the longer term does vary.

Figure 4.1 helps to illustrate the two characteristics of economic growth: positive over the longer term, but volatile in the short term. It plots, from the mid-1950s, the level of real GDP in the UK (left-hand side) alongside the annual rate of economic growth (right-hand side).

Whether it is the volatility of economic growth in the short term or the average rate of growth over the longer term, the issue of economic growth raises important and challenging questions for both economists and policy-makers. In this chapter we focus on short-term fluctuations in real GDP.

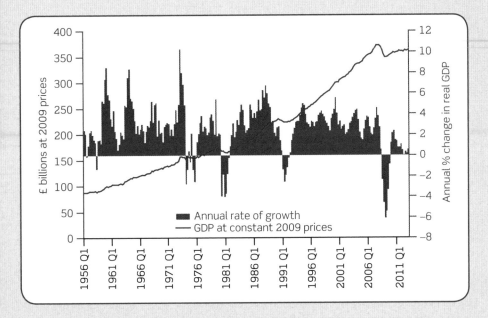

Figure 4.1 Economic growth in the UK.

Source: Based on data from Quarterly National Accounts, Table A2, National Statistics.

→ Revision checklist

What you need to know:

☐ The distinction between short-term and long-term economic growth.

☐ The phases of the business cycle.

☐ How fluctuations in aggregate demand (*AD*) can contribute to the business cycle.

☐ Explanations as to why the component expenditures of aggregate demand fluctuate.

☐ How to analyse the short-run and long-run effects on real GDP originating from a change in aggregate demand after incorporating the effects of expectations and wage contracts.

☐ How fluctuations in aggregate supply (*AS*) can contribute to the business cycle.

☐ Explanations as to why aggregate supply fluctuates.

☐ How to explain how the concept of the business cycle differs between mainstream economics and real business cycle theory.

Assessment question

Can you answer this essay-type question? Guidelines on answering the question are presented at the end of this chapter.

What explanations can economists provide to help understand why short-term economic growth rates are so volatile?

What is the business cycle?

Characterising the business cycle

Rates of short-term economic growth are highly variable. It is this fact that gives rise to the concept of a **business cycle**. If rates of growth ceased to fluctuate then the business cycle would effectively cease too. We can characterise an economy by its position in the business cycle. Figure 4.2 shows a simplified representation of the business cycle. It is nothing more than a characterisation of the business cycle. It shows the *level* of actual output (real GDP) fluctuating around the economy's potential output. As we have seen (Chapter 3), potential output is the level of output when the economy's resources are employed at normal levels of utilisation.

Key definition

Business cycle

The fluctuations in real GDP that result from variations in short-term rates of economic growth.

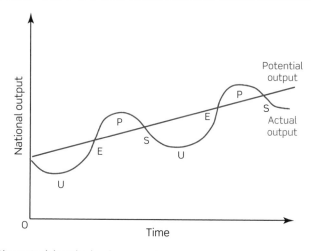

Figure 4.2 Characterising the business cycle.

Assessment advice

It is important in using the diagram characterising the business cycle (Figure 4.2) for you explain that it is merely a representation of the business cycle. Take care not to give the impression that real GDP behaves just as in the diagram! Equally, you may also want to consider whether potential output is really likely to grow at a constant rate as implied by the linear line in the diagram.

Several characteristics of the business cycle can be gleaned from Figure 4.2. First, the path of actual output (real GDP) can be upwards or downwards and so growth can be positive or negative. Second, the slope of the real GDP series varies. This is consistent with rates of growth being variable. Third, the level of output can rise above its potential level causing a positive output gap (see Chapter 3) or fall below its potential level causing a negative output gap.

We can also use Figure 4.2 to identify four phases of the business cycle: *upturn* (U), *expansion* (E), *peaking-out* (P) and *slowdown* (S). In the upturn, growth returns to the economy, but it is during the expansionary phase that growth is most rapid. During the peaking-out phase, growth again slows, while in the slow-down phase there is little growth or possibly a decline in output. The slowdown phase may even see the economy slide into recession. A **recession** occurs when the economy's output contracts for two or more consecutive quarters.

Following the financial crisis of the late 2000s the UK economy was thought to have experienced a **double-dip recession**. This occurs when a country goes back into recession only shortly after coming out of recession. This helps to make the point that, in practice, business cycles are less regular in their shape than is depicted in Figure 4.2. They also tend to differ in their amplitude and so in the extent of the output gaps. In the example, we analyse the depth and duration of UK recessions since the mid-1950s.

Key definitions

Recession
Declining output (real GDP) for two or more consecutive quarters.

Double-dip recession
An economy experiencing recession only shortly after exiting a recession.

Recap

The business cycle is the name given to fluctuations in real GDP around its potential level. During the business cycle the rate of economic growth fluctuates.

Test yourself

Q1. What is meant by potential output?

Q2. Redraw Figure 4.2 to show the path of real GDP if, after temporarily resuming growth, the economy experiences a double-dip recession.

Examples & evidence

The depth and duration of UK recessions

One approach to characterising recessions is to consider what we may term the three 'Ds' of recession: their *depth*, their *duration* and their *determinants*. The last of these relates to the causes or explanations. However, we focus here on the depth and duration of recessions.

To identify a recession we need to observe two or more consecutive quarters where real GDP has declined; that is, where economic growth has been negative. To do so requires quarterly data on real GDP. In the chart below we plot the quarterly rates of economic growth observed in the UK since the mid-1950s. They tell us by what percentage real GDP grew in each quarter of the calendar year. The average quarterly rate of increase in real GDP over the period is 0.63 per cent.

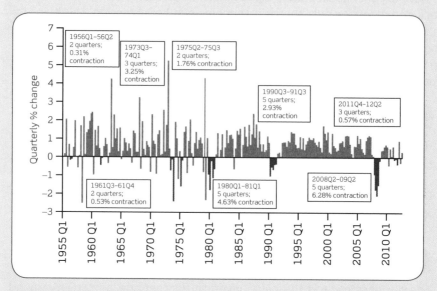

UK recessions since 1955.
Source: Based on data from Quarterly National Accounts, Table A2, National Statistics.

From the chart, we are able to identify eight recessions. We can then distinguish between them by depth and duration. The duration of the recession is simply the number of quarters during which real GDP declined. We can identify three recessions that lasted for five quarters: early 1980s, early 1990s and late 2000s. In contrast, three recessions lasted for the minimum duration of two quarters: 1956, 1961 and 1975. However, in the case of the 1975 recession, it followed closely on the back of the 1973–4 recession. This is an example of a double-dip recession.

The depth of the recessions refers to the amount of lost output. To calculate this we compare the size of real GDP in the quarter immediately prior to the start of the recession with the level in the last quarter of the recession. We can then calculate the percentage decline in real GDP. The figures reveal that the deepest recession in the past 60 years or so was that in the late 2000s when real GDP fell by nearly 6.3 per cent. In contrast, the shallowest recession was during 1956 when real GDP fell by 0.3 per cent.

Questions

1. Explain what you understand by 'the three Ds of recession'. Can you think of other ways by which we could distinguish periods of recession?

2. Using the data in the chart, rank the recessions in descending order of depth (amount of lost output).

International business cycles

Over time, the interdependence or interconnectedness of countries has increased. We will return to this theme later (see Chapter 7). This interdependence occurs primarily because of trade between countries and because of the global nature of financial markets and institutions. This interdependency means that we frequently observe similarities between countries' business cycles and the business cycles exhibited by the global economy. We observe, for instance, coincidence between turning points in economic growth. This was especially apparent in the late 2000s when the financial crisis spread like a contagion.

Figure 4.3 shows the annual rates of economic growth in a sample of developed countries. Although there is evidence that domestic factors do 'shape' countries' business cycles, we do observe points in time, such as 1973–4 and the late 2000s, when different countries' business cycles appear very closely aligned. The **international business cycle** is therefore frequently mirrored by the business cycles of national economics.

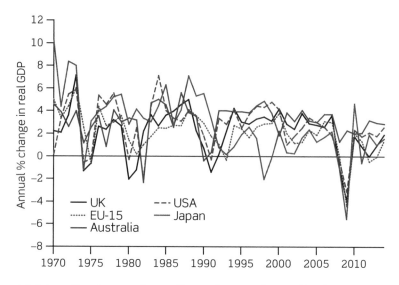

Figure 4.3 International comparisons of annual economic growth rates.

Note: Figures from 2012 are forecasts; EU-15 = the member countries of the European Union prior to 1 May 2004.

Source: AMECO Database, European Commission, DGECFIN.

Key definition

International business cycle

Fluctuations in global output that are frequently mirrored by national economies.

Fluctuations in aggregate demand

Shifts of the *AD* curve

Having identified that short-term economic growth rates are variable we consider a range of *possible* explanations. In doing so, we are trying to understand why economies are inherently unstable. Inevitably, given the seriousness of this issue, different economists have different explanations and consequently different 'remedies'.

One of the reasons that economists offer different views on the causes of fluctuations in real GDP is that they hold different views about how economies work. Equally, they have different views about the role that governments should play in trying to stabilise the economy. Some argue that governments can be a major contributor to fluctuating growth rates. In contrast, others argue that governments have an important role to play in reducing economic volatility.

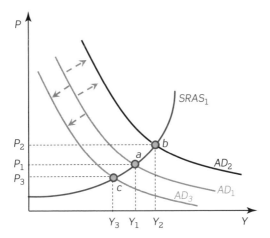

Figure 4.4 Fluctuations in aggregate demand.

Despite these differences, mainstream analysis continues to focus on fluctuations in real GDP originating from fluctuations in *aggregate demand*. We can use the *AD–AS* model to help illustrate this. Because aggregate demand is constantly shifting, the *AD* curve in Figure 4.4 is constantly shifting too.

Over the longer term, the shifts in aggregate demand result in the *AD* curve moving to the *right*. This largely reflects the greater prosperity of the purchasers of national output. However, in the short term aggregate demand can increase or decrease. An increase in aggregate demand leads to a rightward shift of the *AD* curve (AD_1 to AD_2) and a fall in aggregate demand causes a leftward shift of the *AD* curve (AD_1 to AD_3). In both cases, the change in aggregate demand is the result of something other than a change in the GDP deflator. A change in the GDP deflator causes a move along the *AD* (and *SRAS*) curve.

✳ Assessment advice

Be sure to construct and label your diagram accurately. Any diagrams you include in your answer need to be integrated into the text to support your answer. Use your diagrams for a purpose.

Figure 4.4 helps to show that the extent to which output changes (the rate of economic growth) and the extent to which the GDP deflator changes (the rate of inflation or deflation) both depend on the size of the change in aggregate demand and on the initial position of the macroeconomy. Furthermore, as we shall see as we go through this chapter, output and price changes also depend on the behaviour of economic agents in *response* to the change in aggregate demand.

But what causes aggregate demand to change in the first place? It is to this question that we now turn.

Assessment advice

The business cycle is the name given to the fluctuations in real GDP caused by the variability in rates of economic growth. The focus of many economic explanations lies with the volatility of aggregate demand. It is therefore important to understand the concept of aggregate demand and the components comprising it, and to develop a 'feel' for the sorts of factors that might affect these expenditure components.

Recap

Mainstream economic analysis focuses on the volatility of aggregate demand in explaining the fluctuations in real GDP.

Test yourself

A _____ in aggregate demand will cause the *AD* curve to shift to the left. The effect will be a _____ in real GDP and a _____ in the GDP deflator.

Household consumption

A good starting point in exploring variations in the rate of growth in aggregate demand is household consumption. This is because household consumption (consumer spending) is the single largest expenditure component of aggregate demand. In the UK about two-thirds of aggregate demand is consumer spending. Therefore, even relatively small shifts in consumer spending can have sizeable effects on aggregate demand and hence on the size of the economy.

We have already discussed possible determinants of consumer spending (see Chapter 2). An obvious starting point is to consider the impact of changes in disposable income, that is post-tax income, on consumption. This can be quantified by the **marginal propensity to consume**, which measures the proportion of a change in disposable income that impacts on consumption. For instance, if disposable income increases by £1 and consumption increases by 80p, the marginal propensity to consume is 0.8.

Evidence suggests that households typically try to 'smooth' their profile of spending so that when viewed over time it is less variable than it otherwise would be (see 'Examples & evidence' in Chapter 2). This is despite fluctuating incomes, reflecting, among other factors, career progression, the age profile or composition of households, or changes in personal circumstances. The act of reducing the variability in consumer spending despite volatile disposable income is known as **consumption smoothing**.

Although the extent of consumption smoothing varies across households, we typically observe greater volatility in the disposable income across the household sector than we do in consumption. Consequently, we tend to observe that the short-term marginal propensity to consume out of changes in disposable income is less than 1. Hence, although changes in disposable income do affect consumer spending and do contribute to the business cycle, their impact is lessened by the extent to which households 'smooth' their spending.

Key definitions

Marginal propensity to consume (*mpc*)
The proportion of an increase in national income spent by households.

Consumption smoothing
The attempt by households to reduce the variability of their spending despite facing volatile incomes.

✳ Assessment advice

Household spending is the largest component by value of aggregate demand. Try to think about your own consumption behaviour and that of your family and friends. What variables affect their spending? Might some of these be important in understanding what causes consumption to grow more or less strongly?

Consumption smoothing is facilitated by the financial system. Households can use financial instruments to supplement incomes either by borrowing (obtaining credit) or by drawing down on previously acquired financial assets. Alternatively, they can use financial instruments to divert current income to the future, thereby postponing spending until a later date. Although, over the longer term, changes in household spending and income will tend to be broadly similar, in the short term, especially the very short term, consumption will often be *less* sensitive to income changes. However, the extent of consumption smoothing can vary and, hence, the short-term impact of income changes on consumer spending will vary too.

There are two major reasons why the degree of consumption smoothing might vary. First, the *willingness* of consumers to smooth their spending changes. For instance, household behaviour is affected by confidence (sentiment) and by expectations of the future. If confidence is low, perhaps because expectations of future income prospects are bleak, households may be less willing to draw on savings or access credit to supplement incomes. Therefore, if the household sector is experiencing low or negative growth in its real disposable income, it might be unwilling to supplement it. Consequently, consumption would be more sensitive to income changes and the path of consumption would track more closely that of disposable income.

Second, the *ability* of households to smooth spending can vary. A key issue here is the willingness of financial institutions to provide credit. For example, if financial institutions tighten credit criteria during periods of weak real income growth, this will negatively impact on consumption growth. In contrast, if banks relax credit criteria during periods of strong real income growth this will help to boost consumption. In both cases, financial institutions could exacerbate the consumption cycle, thereby making consumption more sensitive to income changes.

Recap

Consumption is the largest expenditure component of aggregate demand. Therefore, even relatively small changes in consumer spending can potentially have a significant impact on aggregate demand and, in turn, on output.

Test yourself

Q1. What variables could affect the response by households to a change in their disposable (post-tax) income?

Q2. How would a tightening of banks' credit criteria, such as that seen following the financial crisis of the late 2000s, affect consumer spending?

Investment

The most volatile expenditure component is investment (gross capital formation). As Figure 4.5 helps to show, short-term rates of growth in investment are even more variable than those in the economy as a whole.

One explanation of the volatility in investment is known as the **accelerator theory of investment**. The key idea here is that a large part of business investment is in response to the growth in aggregate demand. Therefore, firms' investment plans are sensitive to the growth in the economy.

When the rate of economic growth increases, firms may need to engage in **induced investment**: investment in physical goods and inputs to help meet the higher demand for final goods and services. Total investment comprises both induced investment and **replacement investment**. The latter recognises that capital goods are subject to wear and tear and, with technological advance,

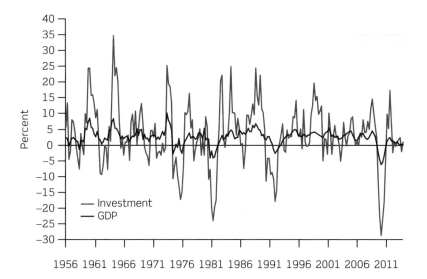

Figure 4.5 Real annual growth rates in UK GDP and investment.

Source: Based on data from Quarterly National Accounts, Table A3, National Statistics.

can become obsolete. The effect of rising economic growth may mean that the rate of increase in total investment is considerably larger than the rate of increase in aggregate demand.

Key definitions

Accelerator theory

A theory to explain the volatility of investment that assumes that the level of investment is dependent on the rate of growth in national income.

Induced investment

Investment by firms in response to increased demand for their goods and services.

Replacement investment

Investment by firms to replace capital because of wear and tear or it becoming obsolete.

When economic growth slows, induced investment falls. Therefore, according to the acceleratory theory, we could observe the economy growing, albeit more slowly, and yet see investment fall because fewer additional capital goods and services are needed. In short, the accelerator theory implies that the level of investment is positively related not to the level of output, but to the *growth* in output.

More generally, the volatility in investment expenditure is unsurprising when one thinks about the vast sums of money that are often involved with investment. The financial commitment for both private- and public-sector investment can be immense. Consider the costs involved in new buildings and office space, in the purchasing of vehicles, machinery and plant or, with government, in major infrastructural projects.

The growth of capital expenditure is likely to be sensitive both to the current macroeconomic environment and to expectations of the economy in the future. Weak business confidence is likely to cause firms to postpone major capital projects, while greater optimism will positively affect the growth of investment. The availability and cost of finance will be other critical considerations too. A reduction in the availability of credit and/or an increase in the cost of finance will negatively impact on levels of investment expenditure.

Recap

Investment expenditure is typically the most volatile expenditure component of aggregate demand. The accelerator theory suggests that the level of investment is dependent on the rate of growth of the economy because a primary purpose of investment is to provide firms with additional productive capacity. Other influences include the price and availability of credit and business confidence.

Test yourself

Q1. Using the accelerator theory, explain why the level of investment might fall even when economic growth is positive.

Q2. Draw up a list of factors that you think might affect private-sector investment. Repeat the exercise for public-sector investment.

Fiscal policy

Automatic stabilisers

Fiscal policy refers to changes in the level of government spending, including welfare expenditures, and rates of taxation. Some elements of spending and taxation have the effect of automatically stabilising the economy during the phases of the business cycle. This is because they are dependent on economic conditions. Therefore, these elements of fiscal policy are known as **automatic stabilisers**.

For instance, as national income rises, the amount of tax paid will tend to rise. Tax receipts are a withdrawal of income from the circular flow of income (see

Chapter 2) and so their rise will help to 'smooth' the business cycle by reducing the increase in real GDP. The extent to which the amount of tax increases will depend on how *progressive* taxation is. The overall progressiveness of taxation is measured by the ratio of the amount of tax (T) collected to national income (Y), that is T/Y. The more progressive the taxation, the more the tax receipts increase when national income increases.

A government's welfare expenditures can also help to reduce the fluctuations in real GDP. With rising national income, income-related benefits and the total amount paid in unemployment benefits will tend to fall.

Key definition

Automatic stabilisers

Changes in the level of government spending and in payments of tax resulting from changes in national income that help to stabilise the economy.

Discretionary fiscal policy

Deliberate changes in levels of government expenditure or in rates of taxation are known as **discretionary fiscal policy**. Discretionary fiscal policy, just as with the role of governments more generally in an economy, is highly contentious. There are economists who argue that governments tend to exacerbate the business cycle by making the fluctuations in real GDP larger.

A major reason for the different views on how actively governments should affect the level of aggregate demand through fiscal policy is quite simply that there are very different views on how economies work. Some economists argue that markets tend towards equilibrium fairly quickly – at least if governments do not overly interfere! Put another way, there are inherent mechanisms at work in the economy that will result in the economy's output moving towards its potential level. However, other economists argue that it can take the economy a considerable amount of time to move towards its potential output. They argue that governments can help the economy towards its potential output.

It is also claimed that governments might have an incentive to use policy tools, like levels of expenditure and rates of taxation, to affect the path of the economy in order to try and affect their own chances of re-election. This can cause a **political business cycle** where the business cycle is shaped by the time elapsed between elections. At its most extreme, we would tend to observe higher rates of growth immediately prior to elections and lower rates of growth (perhaps even negative) in the early part of a new government's period in power.

Another concern expressed over discretionary fiscal policy concerns **time lags**, which might magnify the fluctuations in real GDP. One type of lag with fiscal policy occurs in its *implementation*. Fiscal changes are usually undertaken as part of annual 'Budgets' which require parliamentary approval. Another key lag is the time that it takes for the policy changes to affect the macroeconomy. Furthermore, these changes can often be difficult to *forecast*, not least because they crucially depend on the responses of economic agents.

Key definitions

Discretionary fiscal policy

Deliberate changes to the level of government expenditure and/or rates of taxation.

Political business cycle

The idea that governments deliberately attempt to affect the economy, including the path of real GDP, to increase the likelihood of their re-election.

Time lags

Lags in the implementation and impact of fiscal policy that might result in greater fluctuations of real GDP than would otherwise be the case.

Recap

The impact of governments on the business cycle is very contentious. Some economists advocate that governments should play an active role in managing aggregate demand so as to alleviate fluctuations in real GDP. In contrast, others argue that governments only exacerbate the fluctuations in real GDP and so fiscal policy should be more passive.

Test yourself

Q1. How might time lags associated with fiscal policy make the fluctuations in real GDP larger?

Q2. Is a political business cycle more or less likely if governments have to hold an election at fixed points in time, for example every five years?

Financial system

The financial system is an integral part of the macroeconomy. The well-being and stability of both the financial system and the macroeconomy are very closely tied, something that the financial crisis of the late 2000s demonstrated only too well. The massive expansion of banks' balance sheets over the 1990s and 2000s makes it increasingly important for national economies that banks' balance sheets are managed effectively. As we shall see later (Chapter 5), one response of policy-makers has been to increase the funds that banks must hold to make them more financially resilient.

The financial system channels funds from those with surplus funds to those with deficit funds. It provides both short-term and longer-term credit. Short-term credit allows economic agents to 'fill the gap' when there are temporary shortfalls in income, perhaps when the timing of receipts of income does not perfectly match expenditures.

The willingness of banks to provide this short-term credit impacts on the amount of liquidity that economic agents have and so on their spending power. Consequently, banks can contribute to the business cycle by relaxing or tightening their lending criteria. This happens when they loosen their credit criteria and are more willing to provide credit during periods of strong economic growth and, conversely, tighten credit criteria when economic growth is weakest. The act by financial institutions of contracting and expanding credit depending on the rate of economic growth gives rise to a **credit cycle**. The credit cycle contributes to the amplitude of the business cycle.

Some economists argue that financial institutions are a key ingredient in explaining business cycles. Others point to the stabilising impact on the economy of short-term credit in providing liquidity and enabling economic agents to 'smooth' their spending plans.

Key definition

Credit cycle

The expansion or contraction of credit provided by financial institutions across the business cycle.

Financial institutions and markets provide long-term credit too. They allow, for instance, businesses to undertake investment expenditure. Investment expenditure (I) is a component of aggregate demand. Therefore, if firms find it harder (easier) to access long-term finance, perhaps through loans from banks or a share issue, then this will have a negative (positive) impact on the level of investment and on aggregate demand. In other words, the financial system can contribute to the observed volatility in investment. It is worth noting too that investment affects not only aggregate demand but also aggregate supply. It does so by affecting the economy's stock of capital and, in turn, its potential output. The rate of growth of investment can affect not only short-term economic growth but longer-term economic growth too.

Recap

Financial institutions are an integral part of the economy. They provide short-term and long-term credit. If they relax (tighten) lending criteria when growth is strong (weak) they can exacerbate the business cycle by making the fluctuations in real GDP larger.

Test yourself

Q1. What do you understand by a bank's lending criteria? How might we measure them?

Q2. How can financial institutions help to smooth the business cycle? How can they make the fluctuations in real GDP larger?

✱ Assessment advice

The financial crisis of the late 2000s clearly demonstrated how the financial system can be a destabilising influence on the economy. Yet try to think more generally about the influence of the financial system on economic behaviour and the role that it plays both in contributing to fluctuations in economic growth and in reducing them.

Expectations and contracts

Expectations are important in affecting the behaviour of economic agents. Expectations can affect the level of economic activity. For instance, if households and firms are pessimistic about the prospects for the economy and believe that future real income growth will be weak, this is likely to have a negative effect on their current levels of spending. Consequently, we might see weak consumption growth across households and weak investment growth across firms. The result is that expectations become self-fulfilling, helping to propel the economy down the very path that was expected.

Expectations also play an important role in determining prices, including wage rates. Workers and their representatives will take into account expected future inflation rates when negotiating pay. After all, workers will not want to see the purchasing power of their income fall. In other words, they will want to avoid the rate of price inflation exceeding the rate of wage inflation since this would erode the *real* value of their wages. Price expectations therefore affect the position of the aggregate supply curve.

Some economists emphasise the effect on the economy of tying workers (or other suppliers) to contracts. Wage contracts are often set for periods of at

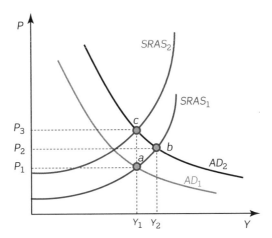

Figure 4.6 Short-term and long-term effects of an increase in aggregate demand.

least one year. Consequently, the effect of unexpected changes in aggregate demand on the economy cannot be readily offset by changes in input prices. In other words, contracts increase the impact of aggregate demand changes on real GDP.

Consider Figure 4.6 and assume that the economy is initially in equilibrium at point a (Y_1, P_1). Now assume that aggregate demand increases. This puts upward pressure on the prices of final goods and so the GDP deflator rises. When workers and other suppliers of inputs are able to incorporate this into their own price demands, such as wage rates, the aggregate supply will move upwards because of higher input prices. The result of higher input prices is to reduce the *real* increase in aggregate demand and, hence, the increase in real GDP. If the SRAS curve moves from $SRAS_1$ to $SRAS_2$, the increase in nominal aggregate demand is totally absorbed by higher prices and so real aggregate demand is unchanged.

Consider now two important issues. First, to what extent will the increase in the GDP deflator resulting from the increase in aggregate demand have been expected? Put another way, how much *unexpected* inflation has actually occurred? The more expected the rise in the GDP deflator, the more likely it is that higher input prices will choke off the rise in aggregate demand by causing the SRAS curve to move upwards.

Second, to what extent can workers and other suppliers of inputs raise their prices even when inflation is expected? For example, if workers are tied to contracts, they may be unable to do much to prevent higher prices eroding their real wages.

These and other questions are important because they affect the extent to which output increases above Y_1 following the increase in aggregate demand. If it takes time for suppliers to offset the impact of the higher GDP deflator by increasing input prices, the economy could be at a point like *b* for some time. On the other hand, if adjustments in aggregate supply occur quite readily then the economy could move from point *a* to *c* quite quickly. *Real* aggregate demand and, hence, real GDP are the same at points *a* and *c*.

 ## Assessment advice

Do not confuse nominal and real aggregate demand. Nominal aggregate demand is the monetary value of the demand for firms' goods and services. Real aggregate demand refers to the volume of demand for firms' goods and services. It is real aggregate demand that is being measured on the horizontal axis of *our AD–AS* diagram.

We could repeat the analysis of Figure 4.6 but this time for a fall in aggregate demand. In this case the GDP deflator falls. Again, questions about the subsequent adjustment process divide economists. Some economists argue that because workers are unlikely to negotiate cuts to their actual (nominal) wages, the decline in real GDP could persist. They would advocate that government considers boosting aggregate demand (see Chapter 3).

Recap

Expectations are a crucial determinant of the behaviour of economic agents. They affect aggregate demand by affecting the propensity of economic agents to spend. They can also affect aggregate supply by affecting the price expectations of the suppliers of inputs, including the wage demands of workers.

Test yourself

Q1. How might pessimistic expectations of personal finances affect the amount of saving by households?

Q2. How does the length of wage contracts affect the extent of fluctuations in real GDP arising from variations in aggregate demand?

Fluctuations in aggregate supply

Shifts of the *AS* curve

As we have seen, much of the economic analysis on the business cycle tends to focus on the fluctuations in output that originate from changes in aggregate demand. Changes in aggregate supply, such as those that follow from

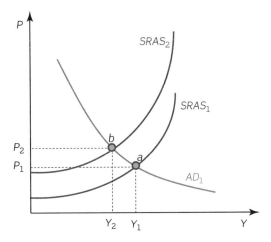

Figure 4.7 Decrease in *SRAS*.

changes in wages, can result from changes in aggregate demand. However, economists recognise that fluctuations in real GDP can originate from changes in aggregate supply.

One commonly cited example is the price of oil. This is not only because of the importance of oil in many production processes, but also because of the variability in its price. For example, between Q1 (quarter 1) of 1973 and Q1 of 1974 the average price of a barrel of crude rose by over 500 per cent. This is an example of a *negative* **supply-side shock**. The effect was to move the *SRAS* curve to the left: at each level of the GDP deflator aggregate supply is reduced.

The possible impact of a negative supply-side shock is illustrated in Figure 4.7. It is drawn assuming that the economy's potential output is unaffected; that is, it becomes vertical at the same level of output. If potential output was reduced, the new *SRAS* curve ($SRAS_2$) would become vertical at a lower level of output (real GDP). Nonetheless, the general conclusion is the same: the short-term macroeconomic equilibrium sees output fall (Y_1 to Y_2) and yet the economy's price level rises (P_1 to P_2). The extent to which prices rise and the level of output falls will depend on the magnitude of the shock and on the responses of economic agents.

A positive supply shock would see the *SRAS* curve move rightwards. The result would be a rise in output and a fall in the GDP deflator. This could be the result of falling input prices (including oil) or a positive **productivity shock**, such as a technological breakthrough, that increases the effectiveness of inputs. Productivity shocks therefore affect the economy's production function, that is the relationship between the economy's inputs and the amount of output. Consequently, they also affect the economy's potential output.

> ## Key definitions
>
> **Supply-side shock**
> A shock that affects the position of the aggregate supply curve by affecting the amount that firms are collectively willing to supply at different price levels.
>
> **Productivity shock**
> A shock that affects the effectiveness of those inputs used in production.

Real business cycle theory

Some economists take a more radical view of business cycles. Real business cycle economists question our original definition of the business cycle as fluctuations in real GDP around potential output. They argue that the observed fluctuations in real GDP are largely fluctuations in potential output itself. They focus their explanations of the business cycle on understanding shifts in the economy's potential output.

Real business cycles are caused by *impulses* that affect potential output. The focus has largely been on impulses originating on the supply side and, in particular, on *productivity shocks*. In other words, the impulses are 'shocks' that affect the productivity of the inputs used in production.

Real business cycle theory argues that the impact on output from the original impulse (shock) persists. This persistence comes from what are called **propagating mechanisms**. For instance, a positive productivity shock raises the general effectiveness of firms' capital stocks. Consequently, it becomes profitable for firms to invest over and above levels needed because of wear and tear or because capital becomes obsolete (replacement investment). The profitability of investment induces firms to invest and so raises the economy's stock of capital per worker. This increase in capital per worker is referred to as **capital deepening** (see Chapter 3). Because of capital deepening, the economy's potential output increases further still. The initial impulse has been propagated by the actions of firms.

> ## Key definitions
>
> **Real business cycles**
> Business cycles caused by shocks to aggregate supply that persist, thereby affecting potential output.

Propagating mechanisms

The name given by real business cycle theorists to the means by which shocks to the economy can have enduring effects.

Capital deepening

An increase in the amount of capital per worker.

✳ Assessment advice

Although we normally think of the business cycle as fluctuations in real GDP around the economy's potential output, real business cycle theory reminds us that potential output may fluctuate too. Revisit Figure 4.2 and think about the consequences of this for our understanding of the business cycle.

Chapter summary – pulling it all together

By the end of this chapter you should be able to:

	Confident ✓	Not confident?
Distinguish between short-term and long-term economic growth		Revise pages 80–82
Characterise the business cycle so as to be able to identify phases of the business cycle		Revise pages 82–85
Show how variations in *AD* cause fluctuations in real GDP with reference to the *AD–AS* model		Revise pages 86–88
Discuss some of the variables that cause the expenditure components of *AD* to fluctuate		Revise pages 88–96
Using the *AD–AS* model, analyse the short-run and long-run effects on output originating from a change in *AD* after incorporating the effects of expectations and wage contracts		Revise pages 96–98
Discuss some of the variables that cause *AS* to fluctuate		Revise pages 98–100

	Confident ✓	Not confident?
Show how variations in *AS* cause fluctuations in real GDP with reference to the *AD–AS* model		Revise pages 98–100
Explain how the concept of the business cycle differs between mainstream economists and real business cycle economists		Revise pages 100–101

Now try the assessment question at the start of this chapter, using the answer guidelines below.

Answer guidelines

✳ Assessment question

What explanations can economists provide to help understand why short-term economic growth rates are so volatile?

Approaching the question

The question provides you with an opportunity to discuss one of the key issues within macroeconomics: *the business cycle.* In addressing the question you have an opportunity to detail several ideas and theories advanced by economists. But you also have ample opportunity to relate them to the real world and to develop arguments. Therefore, in developing your answer try to avoid being too abstract and merely providing a list of ideas.

Important points to include

- **The concept of the business cycle.** At the outset it is important to define clearly what is meant by the business cycle and to distinguish between short-term and long-term economic growth.

- **Fluctuating aggregate demand.** Mainstream economics focuses on the volatility of aggregate demand in causing fluctuations in real GDP. Explore reasons as to why aggregate demand might be volatile. In doing so, embed within your answer relevant theoretical ideas and frameworks.

- **Fluctuations in aggregate supply.** Economists recognise that fluctuations in aggregate supply can also generate fluctuations in real GDP. Explore in your answer where these may come from. Again, embed within your answer relevant theoretical frameworks, for example the *AD–AS* model. Outline the real business cycle perspective that focuses on fluctuations in aggregate supply as the principal driver of the business cycle.

Make your answer stand out

- Try to develop *arguments* linking the various economic ideas and theories. Avoid your answer becoming one long list of potential explanations. End with conclusions.
- Draw on examples and relate to ac*tual events*. Showing an awareness of your domestic and international macroeconomic environment, for instance, can only help to enrich your answer and 'bring it to life'.
- Show your awareness that economists hold *diverging views* on how economies work. Different economists will place differing degrees of importance on different explanations of the business cycle and, in the case of real business cycle theory, even a different definition of the business cycle! Similarly, economists have different views on the role that governments play in mitigating or contributing to the business cycle.
- When using diagrams make sure they are properly explained and help to develop your argument.

Read to impress

Here are some books, articles and other sources that you can use to develop your answers on the topic area.

Books

Griffiths, A. and Wall, S. (2011) *Economics for Business and Management*, 3rd edition, Chapter 10, 'Government policies: instruments and objectives'. Harlow, UK: Pearson Education.

Parkin, M., Powell, M. and Matthews, K. (2012) *Essential Economics*, European edition, Chapter 15, 'The Business Cycle'. Harlow, UK: Pearson Education.

Sloman, J. and Garratt, D. (2013) *Essentials of Economics*, 6th edition, Chapter 9, 'Aggregate supply and growth'. Harlow, UK: Pearson Education.

Journals

Hills, S. and Thomas, R. (2010) The UK recession in context – what do three centuries of data tell us? *Bank of England Quarterly Bulletin*, Q4: 277–91 (www.bankofengland.co.uk/publications/Documents/quarterlybulletin/qb100403.pdf).

Periodicals and newspapers

The Bank of England's *Inflation Report* contains a readable overview of recent patterns in the component expenditures of UK aggregate demand.

The *Office for National Statistics* publishes a range of relevant data and supporting commentaries on the economy. These include releases relating to national income, expenditure and output. Information relating to these topic areas can be accessed at: www.ons.gov.uk/ons/taxonomy/index.html?nscl=National+Income%2C+Expenditure+and+Output.

Financial Times (2012) US growth slows to 1.5%. Robin Harding and James Politi, 27 July.

Financial Times (2012) The US economy is still in a sorry state. Edward Luce, 23 September.

Financial Times (2012) Germany data add to eurozone crisis. James Fontanella-Khan and Chris Bryant, 24 October.

Financial Times (2012) Britain moves out of recession. Sarah O'Connor, 25 October.

Financial Times (2012) GDP growth revised down to 0.9%. Claire Jones, 21 December.

Financial Times (2013) Confidence grows but fears curb spending. Brian Groom, 7 January.

Companion website

Go to the companion website at **www.pearsoned.co.uk/econexpress** to find more revision support online for this topic area.

Notes

Notes

5 Banking, money and monetary policy

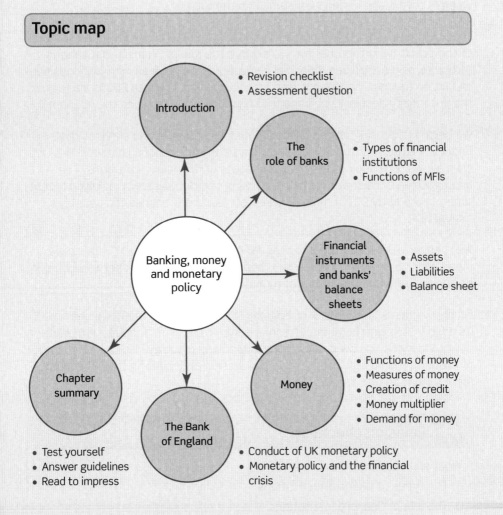

- Introduction
  - Revision checklist
  - Assessment question
- The role of banks
  - Types of financial institutions
  - Functions of MFIs
- Financial instruments and banks' balance sheets
  - Assets
  - Liabilities
  - Balance sheet
- Money
  - Functions of money
  - Measures of money
  - Creation of credit
  - Money multiplier
  - Demand for money
- The Bank of England
  - Conduct of UK monetary policy
  - Monetary policy and the financial crisis
- Chapter summary
  - Test yourself
  - Answer guidelines
  - Read to impress

Banking, money and monetary policy

A printable version of this topic map is available from **www.pearsoned.co.uk/econexpress**

Introduction

Financial institutions play an incredibly important role in our everyday lives. They provide us with an array of products and services that have radically shaped the way that we conduct economic activity. Over time our dependence on the financial system has grown. For instance, individuals can shop with nothing but a piece of plastic, they are able to obtain short-term credit to 'plug the gap' between spending and income and they are able to obtain long-term credit, such as a mortgage to purchase property. Furthermore, as all students know, financial institutions allow us to consume today some of our expected future income or, conversely, to postpone consuming some of our current income, save it and instead consume it in the future.

Financial institutions are important not just for households, but for all sectors of the economy. In this chapter, we explore the role of financial institutions. Although, as we shall see, financial institutions can have an incredibly positive impact on the macroeconomy, the financial crisis of the late 2000s illustrates the potentially destabilising impact of financial institutions on the economy.

We begin by focusing on the types of financial products and services that financial institutions provide and how these affect economic activity. This then allows us to look at the balance sheets of financial institutions. The aggregate balance sheet of the UK banking sector has grown rapidly in recent times. In the early 2010s, it is equivalent to around 5½ times the country's annual GDP.

We then move on to consider money. What constitutes money? How do we measure it? In answering these questions, we will make a link between banks' balance sheets and the supply of money.

Finally, we focus on the Bank of England, the UK's central bank. We see how its relationship with commercial banks is important in its conduct of monetary policy. We focus on how it uses monetary policy to achieve its two core aims of ensuring the stability of the financial system and meeting the UK government's inflation rate target.

 Revision checklist

What you need to know:
- ❑ The types of financial institutions.
- ❑ The role of financial institutions.
- ❑ Financial instruments provided by banks and building societies.

- ❑ What is recorded on the aggregate balance sheets of banks and building societies.
- ❑ The functions of money.
- ❑ Measures of the supply of money.
- ❑ How banks create money.
- ❑ The role of the Bank of England.
- ❑ How the Bank of England conducts monetary policy.

✳ Assessment question

Can you answer this essay-type question? Guidelines on answering the question are presented at the end of this chapter.

What financial instruments are recorded on the aggregate balance sheet of banks and building societies? What role do these financial instruments play in the Bank of England's conduct of monetary policy?

The role of banks

Types of financial institution

Financial institutions are **financial intermediaries**. This means that they act as 'go-betweens' linking those economic agents with deficit financial funds (borrowers) and those with surplus financial funds (savers). Traditionally, we distinguish between two principal types of financial intermediary: monetary financial institutions (MFIs) and other financial corporations (OFCs). However, with the evolution of the financial system this distinction has become increasingly blurred.

Monetary financial institutions are deposit-taking institutions and include familiar names on the high street such as Barclays, HSBC, Lloyds, Royal Bank of Scotland and Santander. In other words, this sector encompasses banks, building societies and central banks (the Bank of England in the UK).

Other financial corporations are non-deposit-taking financial institutions including insurance companies, pension funds and investment vehicles. OFCs typically provide customers with longer-term investment services and, consequently, the sector is referred to as the money-holding sector.

Key definitions

Financial intermediaries

Financial institutions that bring together those economic agents looking to borrow and those looking to save.

Monetary financial institutions

The name given to deposit-taking institutions, including banks, building societies and the central bank.

Other financial corporations

Non-deposit-taking financial institutions, such as insurance companies and pension funds, typically used for longer-term investments.

Functions of MFIs

We focus in this chapter on MFIs, that is on banks, building societies and the central bank. In acting as financial intermediaries, MFIs provide an array of financial products catering for the different needs of their customers. They can design products for borrowers looking for either short-term or long-term credit or for investors looking for short-term or long-term invest-ment products. They can also tailor products to reflect the degree of risk that the customer is prepared to take. The point here is that by pooling the resources of its customer base, MFIs can use their expertise to offer cus-tomers better terms than would be the case if the customer, say a saver, had to seek out another individual, say a borrower, willing to engage in a mutually agreeable deal.

MFIs are able to spread risks by lending to a large number of people. This is known as **risk transformation**. It allows a greater number of economic agents to access credit, either short term or long term, than would otherwise be the case and at terms that are more favourable.

MFIs enable payments to be made without the need for cash. Instead funds can be transferred electronically between the bank accounts of the purchaser and the seller. Where this involves different banks, funds are transferred between the **reserve balances** of the banks held at the Bank of England. In effect, these reserve balances act as the current accounts of banks that can be used as a means of settlements between banks.

MFIs are an important source of **liquidity** for the economy, allowing economic agents to choose the degree to which they hold their stock of wealth in liquid form. This means that they can provide customers with a readily accessible source of funds with little risk. The more liquid a financial product is, the more quickly it can be turned into a sum of cash of known value. MFIs can provide liquidity in two main ways. First, they do so through deposit accounts. Second, they provide access to credit. The latter enables households, businesses, governments and even other financial institutions to 'bridge the gap' between their desired spending and their receipts of income.

Key definitions

Risk transformation

The 'spreading of risk' by financial institutions by lending to a large number of customers.

Reserve balances

Accounts held by commercial banks at the Bank of England that act as a form of current account for banks and that allow the settlement of payments between banks.

Liquidity

The ease with which a financial product can be turned into a sum of cash of known value.

In providing longer-term borrowing opportunities MFIs contribute to the funds that businesses need for capital projects. Capital spending helps to boost not only aggregate demand (*AD*) but also aggregate supply (*AS*) and the economy's potential output (see Chapter 3). The growth of potential output is crucial to an economy's long-term growth and prosperity. It causes the *AS* curve to shift rightwards over time as the economy's productive potential increases.

Households too can benefit from longer-term borrowing, particularly homeowners who obtain a mortgage in order to purchase property. The performance of the housing and mortgage markets is closely linked. The longer-term expansion of owner-occupation has gone hand in hand with the growth in size of residential mortgages on banks' balance sheets. The more restricted lending activities of banks following the financial crisis of the late 2000s hit the UK housing market hard, with the level of transactions contracting sharply.

Assessment advice

The financial products offered by banks and building societies do affect our economic well-being. For instance, credit can affect the level of both *AD* and *AS*. Try both to draw on real-world examples and to use model frameworks like the *AD–AS* model to illustrate their importance.

In providing a range of financial products and services, MFIs engage in a process of **maturity transformation**. The typical length or maturity date of loans made by MFIs will be longer than that of the deposits made with MFIs. Indeed, with the most liquid of deposits customers can have access to their funds without notice. Because MFIs are borrowing 'short' (deposits) and lending 'long' (loans) they have a maturity mismatch on their balance sheets.

Key definition

Maturity transformation

The process by which financial institutions borrow short from depositors and lend long to borrowers.

In 'normal times', with a large customer base and confidence in the financial soundness of the MFI, the average daily withdrawals from deposits is roughly matched by customers' payments into their accounts. Furthermore, where there is a mismatch between a bank's monetary flows, causing either a deficit or surplus of funds, the bank can engage with other commercial banks or with the Bank of England in short-term borrowing or lending. This is how the Bank of England exercises general control over interest rates in the economy. The bank rate is the rate at which the Bank of England is prepared to enter into short-term lending to MFIs. It is the interest rate agreed at the monthly meeting of the Bank's Monetary Policy Committee and, hence, is also known as the policy rate. This is discussed in more detail below.

The financial crisis of the late 2000s shook the financial sector. Confidence in financial institutions waned. In the case of Northern Rock we witnessed a 'run on the bank' with customers looking to withdraw their money in large numbers. We also observed the interbank market 'dry up' as banks became reluctant to lend to each other, fearing that banks might default on their loans. In response, the Bank of England had to lend huge sums of liquid funds to financial institutions. At the same time, the government injected capital into ailing financial institutions, such as Royal Bank of Scotland and the Lloyds Banking Group, and, in doing so, ended up owning large stakes.

Recap

Monetary financial institutions (MFIs) are deposit-taking institutions. They engage in maturity transformation providing both liquid deposits and longer-term borrowing opportunities. They are able to do so because of their large number of customers, which also enables them to spread their risks.

Financial instruments and banks' balance sheets

Banks and building societies provide a range of **financial instruments**. These are financial claims, either by customers on the MFI or by the MFI on its customers. The customers of MFIs include households, non-bank firms, other MFIs, OFCs, the public sector and foreign residents.

A financial institution's liabilities are those financial instruments involving a financial claim on the financial institution itself. Its liabilities largely comprise deposits. Its assets are financial instruments involving a financial claim on a third party. Therefore, its assets comprise various types of loans.

Key definition

Financial instruments

Financial products resulting in one party having a financial claim over another.

Liabilities

The principal liabilities of an MFI are its customers' deposits. This means that the customers have a claim on these deposits. There are four major types of deposit:

- **Sight deposits**. Sight deposits can be withdrawn on demand by the depositor without penalty and include current accounts.
- **Time deposits**. Time deposits require notice of withdrawal, but typically pay a higher rate of interest than sight accounts.
- **Certificates of deposit** (CDs). A form of time deposit by firms, including financial institutions, for which MFIs issue a certificate. These certificates can be bought and sold, making the deposit more liquid for the depositor. The use of CDs has grown rapidly in recent years.
- **Sale and repurchase agreements (repos)**. The *sale* of financial assets, such as government bonds (gilts), to other financial institutions, including the Bank of England, in exchange for cash. The financial institution then agrees to *repurchase* its assets at a fixed (higher) price on a fixed date, for example a week later.

Key definitions

Sight deposits
Deposits that can be withdrawn on demand without penalty.

Time deposits
Deposits where notice of withdrawal is needed or where a penalty is incurred for withdrawal.

Certificates of deposit
A form of time deposit where the depositor is issued with a tradable certificate.

Sale and repurchase agreements (repos)
Secured loans where the borrower sells assets, such as government bonds, in exchange for the deposit of cash and agrees to buy the assets back at a fixed price on a fixed date.

As well as deposits, banks have financial claims originating from their shareholders. The difference here, though, is that shareholders cannot take their money out of banks. **Share capital** provides a source of funding to meet sudden increases in withdrawals from depositors and to cover bad debts.

Key definition

Share capital
A long-term source of finance obtained by issuing shares that gives ownership rights to the holders.

Assets

The assets of an MFI are its financial claims on others. We can identify four main categories of assets:

- *Balances at the Bank of England:*
  - **Reserve balances**. The most significant balances are known as reserve balances. These are like the banks' own current accounts and enable banks to settle payments with other banks. Prior to the financial crisis, reserves kept within an agreed range were remunerated at the bank rate, that is the interest rate agreed at the monthly meeting of the Bank of England's Monetary Policy Committee and the rate at which the Bank of England would be prepared to lend to MFIs. In 2009 all reserves began to be remunerated at the bank rate (see below).

- **Cash ratio deposits**. MFIs must also deposit a small fraction of their assets as cash ratio deposits with the Bank of England. These cannot be drawn on demand and earn no interest.

- *Short-term lending:*
  - **Market loans**. These involve interbank lending. The term or duration of the lending varies. First, there is money lent 'at call' which is reclaimable on demand or at 24 hours' notice. Second, there is money lent for periods of up to one year. Third, lending can take place through certificates of deposits (CDs), with the depositor issued with a tradable certificate (see above).
  - **Bills of exchange**. These are short-term IOUs issued by companies (commercial bills) or by government (Treasury bills). Bills are sold 'at discount', which means that they are sold below their face value before then being redeemed on maturity at their face value.
  - **Reverse repos**. A repo is a form of lending using financial instruments, such as gilts, as a form of security. The assets held as security by the depositing bank are known as 'reverse repos'.
  - **Advances**. These are ongoing or long-term credit facilities to households and to businesses. These include overdrafts, outstanding balances on credit card accounts, fixed-term loans and mortgages.

- *Investments:* Financial institutions make investments. These include bonds that are longer-term IOUs issued by companies (corporate bonds) and government (gilts). Bonds pay a fixed sum (coupon) each year as interest. Bonds are a tradable financial instrument that can be bought and sold.

Key definitions

Market loans

Short-term loans from other banks and financial institutions.

Bills of exchange

Short-term debt instruments sold at discount but redeemed by the issuer at face value.

Reverse repos

The assets, such as government bonds, purchased as part of a repo operation.

Advances

Longer-term credit facilities for households and businesses, including long-term loans like residential mortgages.

Assessment advice

It is important to show your understanding of the key financial instruments recorded on a bank's balance sheet. In particular, this means reflecting on their economic significance, the parties involved and the impact they have on the bank's balance sheet.

Balance sheet

The aggregate balance sheet of banks and building societies allows us to look at the significance of the financial instruments we have just introduced. A summary balance sheet of UK MFIs (excluding the Bank of England) is shown in Table 5.1. Around three-quarters of the sector's liabilities comprise sight and time deposits while over half of its assets comprise advances.

Figure 5.1 helps to show how the aggregate balance sheet of banks and building societies grew rapidly through the 2000s. At the start of 1998 the aggregate balance sheet was worth £2.6 trillion, the equivalent of 310 per cent

Table 5.1 Aggregate balance sheet of UK banks and building societies (end of November 2012).

Sterling liabilities	£bn	%	Sterling assets	£bn	%
Sight deposits	1,252.3	34.2	Notes and coins	9.9	0.3
Time deposits	1,452.2	39.7	Cash ratio deposits	2.4	0.1
CDs and other short-term papers	151.6	4.1	Reserve balances	280.3	7.6
Repos	286.7	7.8	Loans	567.3	15.3
Capital and other internal funds	450.1	12.3	Bills	22.6	0.6
Other liabilities	65.0	1.8	Reverse repos	252.5	6.8
			Advances	1,993.0	53.7
			Investments	485.5	13.1
			Other assets	94.9	2.6
Total sterling liabilities	3,657.9	100.0	Total sterling assets	3,708.5	100.0
Foreign currency liabilities	4,316.2		Total foreign currency assets	4,265.5	
Total liabilities	7,974.1		Total assets	7,974.0	

Note: Data are not seasonally adjusted.

Source: Based on data in Bankstats (Monetary and Financial Statistics) – November 2012, Bank of England, 4 January 2013.

of GDP. By the start of 2008, the balance sheet had grown to £8 trillion, the equivalent of around six times GDP. During the early 2010s the aggregate balance sheet remained around the £8 trillion mark.

Although the growth in the balance sheet during the 2000s was, in hindsight, a cause for concern, so too was its changing composition. Financial institutions were making greater use of wholesale lending and borrowing, that is transactions with other financial institutions. This was on a global scale, allowing the balance sheet to expand at a rate that would not have been possible if banks had relied on retail deposits for the funding of their lending activities.

One particular development that fuelled the growth in lending was **securitisation**. Securitisation occurs when a financial institution pools some of its assets, such as residential mortgages, and sells them to investors, largely other financial institutions. It can then use the funds for further advances. The investors are purchasing bonds, known as collateralised debt obligations (CDOs). Their income stream originates from the payments of interest and capital on the securitised assets.

Key definition

Securitisation

Where assets backed by regular cash flows are turned into tradable securities.

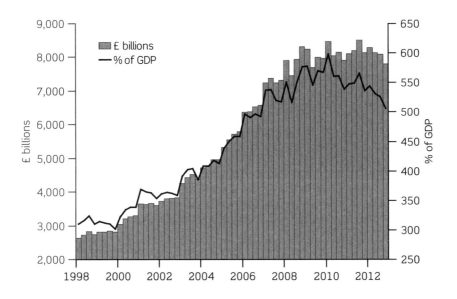

Figure 5.1 Aggregate balance sheet of UK banks and building societies.
Sources: Data showing liabilities of banks and building societies based on series LPMALOA and RPMTBJF (up to the end of 2009) and RPMB3UQ (from 2010) from *Statistical Interactive Database* (Bank of England). Data published 2 April 2013. Data are not seasonally adjusted. GDP data from Quarterly National Accounts (Office for National Statistics). GDP figures are the sum of the latest four quarters.

With more wholesale funds and more long-term credit extended, the composition of the balance sheets developed in three important ways. First, the **liquidity ratio** of banks decreased. The liquidity ratio is the proportion of banks' assets held in liquid form. Second, with an increase in the use of bond financing relative to the issue of ordinary share capital, **gearing (or leverage)** increased. Third, the balance sheets of banks had become increasingly internationalised as financial claims involving foreign residents grew. The overall effect was to leave banks more exposed to their creditors, wherever in the world they were, and with insufficient loss-absorbing capacity if borrowers defaulted on their loans.

Key definitions

Liquidity ratio

The proportion of a financial institution's total assets held in liquid form, that is liquid assets/total assets.

Gearing (or leverage)

The ratio of debt capital to share capital.

Examples & evidence

Securitisation

Securitisation allows financial institutions to bundle more illiquid assets, such as residential mortgages, and transform them into tradable securities that can be sold to investors. This helped individual institutions to secure the liquidity to expand lending activities.

The chart opposite shows the growth of securitisation by UK MFIs (monetary financial institutions) during the 2000s. There was a strong demand among investors for the collateralised debt obligations (CDOs) resulting from securitisation. The attraction of these fixed-income products was that they were perceived as being low risk and yet capable of yielding higher returns than other financial instruments with similar risk ratings.

Through 2006, US interest rates were rising. The result was an increase in the number of households defaulting on residential mortgages. This was a particular problem in the sub-prime market, the market for higher-risk households with poor credit ratings. Consequently, some of the income flows behind the CDOs dried up. Because of the global nature of the market for CDOs, the contagion was on a global scale.

As we can see from the chart, the market for securitised assets collapsed. In 2009, MFIs had to buy back their unsold debt portfolios from financial intermediaries. The market saw only a most modest recovery in the early 2010s.

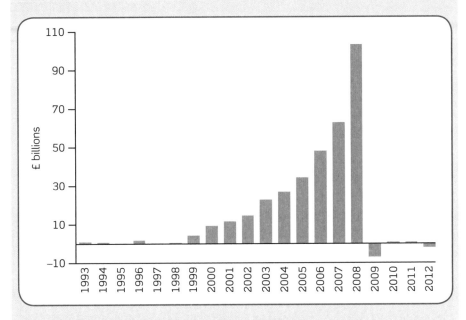

Net securitisations/acquisitions of lending to individuals.
Note: Negative totals indicate acquisition of debt portfolios.
Sources: Based on data from *Statistical Interactive Database* (sum of series LPQB3XE and LPQB3HK), Bank of England (data published 2 April 2013).

Questions

1. What types of assets can be securitised?
2. How did securitisation help to make the financial crisis global?

The need for banks to manage their balance sheets more effectively has been a key element of the subsequent international regulatory response to the financial crisis. The Basel Committee on Banking Supervision has strengthened banks' capital adequacy requirements. **Capital adequacy** is the ratio of a bank's reserves and share capital to its risk-weighted assets. The new 'Basel III' capital requirements will be phased in by 2019 and require banks to hold proportionately more reserves and share capital. The aim is to ensure that in the face of people and businesses defaulting on their loans, banks will have greater loss-absorbing capacity.

Key definition

Capital adequacy

The ratio of a bank's capital to its total assets, where the assets are weighted by their level of risk.

Recap

The balance sheets of banks and building societies are a record of their holdings of financial instruments comprising both liabilities and assets. The aggregate balance sheet of UK banks and building societies has grown massively in recent times. This growth was propelled, in part, by a greater use of wholesale funding, including the securitisation of assets. The financial crisis saw banks with inadequate levels of loss-absorbing capacity. Banks will be required to meet higher capital adequacy targets as part of the new Basel III accord.

Test yourself

Q1. Identify the key liabilities and assets of banks and building societies.

Q2. Why might securitisation cause banks to take more risks?

Money

Functions of money

Ask someone what the main purpose of money is and they are likely to tell you that it is to buy and sell goods and services. This is the idea that money acts as a **medium of exchange**. But money has two other basic functions. First, it acts as a means of evaluation. This means that it allows us to compare the worth of a whole range of goods and services and assets. It even allows us to compare the wealth of nations. Second, money is a means of **storing wealth**. People wish to hold a proportion of their stock of wealth in money. Money is a means by which people can save and add to their existing stock of wealth.

Key definitions

Medium of exchange

The characteristic of money as an acceptable means of payment in economic transactions.

Store of wealth

The ability of economic agents to hold their wealth as money and be able to purchase goods and services in the future.

Measures of the money supply

The narrowest definition of money consists solely of notes and coins in circulation outside of the central bank. This is known as **narrow money**. Figure 5.2 shows the stock of notes and coins in circulation. At the end of 1970, the stock of notes and coins in circulation stood at almost £4 billion, the equivalent of around 7½ per cent of GDP. By the end of 2012, the stock had risen to close on £65 billion, but which as a share of GDP was now only 4 per cent.

Another important narrow measure of money used in the UK includes both notes and coin in circulation with the public and banks' reserve balances at the central bank. In the UK, since May 2006, banks' reserve accounts are interest bearing. Figure 5.3 shows the stock of notes and coins in circulation and banks' reserve balances from 2007. The figure shows a marked increase in reserve balances held by MFIs from 2009. As we shall see in the next section, this coincided with quantitative easing. This was the Bank of England's programme of asset purchases (largely government bonds) in exchange for central bank reserves.

Broader measures of money include many of the deposits on banks' balance sheets. Over time, it has become easier for customers to access funds readily

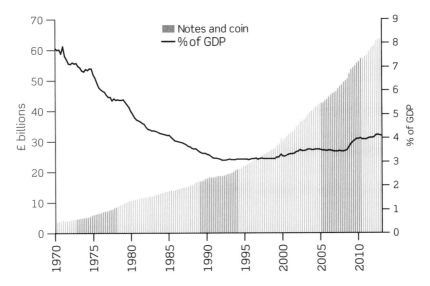

Figure 5.2 Stock of notes and coins (narrow money).
Note: Notes and coins data are seasonally adjusted.
Sources: Notes and coins series (LPMAVAB) from *Statistical Interactive Database*, Bank of England. (data published 3 April 2013); GDP data from *Quarterly National Accounts*, National Statistics.

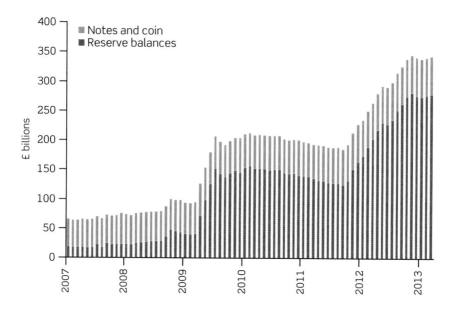

Figure 5.3 Stock of notes and coins and reserve balances.
Note: Data are not seasonally adjusted
Source: Based on series LPMBL22 (reserves) and LPMAVAA (notes and coins) from *Statistical Interactive Database*, Bank of England (data published 3 April 2013).

from different types of deposit accounts including time as well as sight deposits. The boundaries between money and near-money have been blurred.

The UK's principal measure of **broad money** is known as M4. It relates to the money holdings of the UK non-bank private sector, sometimes known as the M4 private sector. The M4 private sector includes households, private non-financial businesses and OFCs, such as pension funds and insurance companies. The financial instruments counting as money are notes and coins, sterling deposits and other short-term sterling-denominated financial instruments issued by banks and building societies with a maturity of up to five years.

Figure 5.4 shows the stock of M4 since 1970. In 1970, the stock of M4 was close to £25 billion, the equivalent of 50 per cent of GDP. By 2012, despite a fall following the financial and economic crisis of the late 2000s, the stock of M4 had risen to £2.1 trillion, the equivalent of 135 per cent of GDP.

Key definitions

Narrow money

Notes and coins in circulation outside the Bank of England.

Broad money

The notes and coins held by the non-bank private sector along with its holdings of financial instruments with a maturity of up to five years.

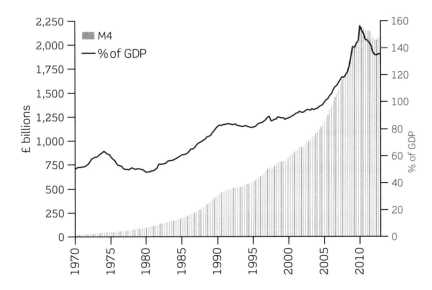

Figure 5.4 Stock of M4.
Note: M4 data are seasonally adjusted
Sources: M4 series LPQAUYN from *Statistical Interactive Database*, Bank of England (data published 2 April 2013); GDP data from *Quarterly National Accounts*, National Statistics.

Recap

There are two main functions of money: as a medium of exchange and a store of wealth. In measuring the stock of wealth we distinguish between 'narrow' and 'broad' measures of money. The narrowest definition of money consists solely of notes and coins in circulation. The UK's broad money measure is known as M4. It includes the notes and coins in circulation and the deposits (with a maturity of up to five years) of the non-bank private sector.

Test yourself

Q1. Why is narrow money also known as high-powered money?

Q2. What connection is there between the balance sheets of banks and building societies and the M4 measure of the money supply?

The creation of credit

A major component of broad money is the deposits on banks' balance sheets. Therefore, an increase in deposits will tend to increase the amount of broad money. However, banks can affect the growth in deposits through their willingness to provide credit. The process of **credit creation** affects the rate of growth of the money supply.

> **Key definition**
>
> **Credit creation**
> The process by which banks increase the money supply through the provision of credit.

Consider the case where government increases its purchases (*G*), perhaps to increase aggregate demand (*AD*). The government will pay for these expenditures by drawing on its account with the Bank of England. Those receiving the cheques will then deposit them with their own bank. Commercial banks will then present them to the Bank of England which will credit their reserve accounts accordingly. Two things have happened so far. First, there has been an expansion of the aggregate balance sheet of banks with an increase in deposits (liabilities) matched by an increase in banks' reserve balances (assets). Second, the mix of assets has changed. The share of liquid assets in total assets has increased. This means that the banking system is operating with a higher liquidity ratio.

The higher liquidity ratio may cause banks to use a proportion of their extra reserves as a source of additional lending to customers. Consequently, banks change the mix of their assets to seek more profitable lending opportunities. As these loans get spent, deposits are created and, at the same time, the reserve accounts of banks at the Bank of England are being duly credited. Therefore, the additional loans reappear in the banking system's reserve accounts.

The aggregate balance sheet of the banking system has expanded again: additional loans (assets) and additional deposits (liabilities). The liquidity ratio across the banking system will now have fallen back because of the additional loans (advances). However, as banks' reserve accounts have been credited because of the additional deposits, the liquidity ratio will not have fallen back to its original level. Therefore, the banking system is able to fund additional loans. This means that the process of additional loans and, in turn, additional deposits is likely to be repeated until eventually the liquidity ratio will have fallen back to a level at which banks wish to operate. In the meantime, the balance sheet and the broad money supply have expanded.

Money multiplier

The reality of credit creation by banks and its impact on broad money is, of course, more complicated than described above. We can identify a series of factors that affect the degree of credit creation and, in turn, the growth of broad money:

- *Liquidity ratio*. As we have seen, this measures the proportion of liquid assets in total assets. The liquidity ratio with which banks operate will vary. Because of the financial crisis of the late 2000s, banks chose to hold a higher liquidity ratio. The impact of a higher liquidity ratio is, other things remaining constant, to reduce the rate of growth of broad money.

- *Aggregate amount of reserves.* The monopoly supplier of reserves (central bank money) is the Bank of England. It can exercise control over monetary policy through its supply of reserves. Although individual banks can engage in interbank lending and borrowing, the Bank of England affects the aggregate amount of reserves. This affects interest rates. For instance, an increase in the demand for credit will, all other things remaining constant, put upward pressure on the interbank interest rates and on the rates at which the public can borrow from financial institutions.

- *Demand for money.* Money is one way in which economic agents hold wealth. If the recipients of funds generated through the expansion of credit decide to hold them *outside* the banking system, perhaps as notes and coins, in goods and services or in less liquid long-term financial assets, this will reduce the extent of credit creation. (We consider the demand for money below.)

One way of monitoring the extent of credit creation is through the **money multiplier**. This measures the rise in broad money for a rise in narrow money. In the UK, we may calculate this by the *change* in M4 relative to the *change* in the sum of notes and coins in circulation and banks' reserve accounts.

Key definition

Money multiplier
The number of times greater is the change in broad money following a change in narrow money.

If we want to get a clearer sense of the longer-term relationship between the stocks of broad money and narrow money, we can look at the ratio of the two, that is at the *level* of broad money relative to the *level* of narrow money.

Figure 5.5 plots the ratio of the stock of M4 (broad money) to the stock of notes and coins and banks' reserve accounts. We observe a rise in the ratio of broad to narrow money through the 1980s before remaining relatively constant through much of the 1990s and into the early part of the 2000s. It then rises again up to the financial crisis before declining markedly. The falls in 2009 and again in 2011 and 2012 coincided with the Bank of England's programme of quantitative easing which resulted in a massive expansion of banks' reserve accounts. The increase in the narrower measure of money was not matched by the same proportionate increase in broad money as banks chose to keep larger reserve accounts.

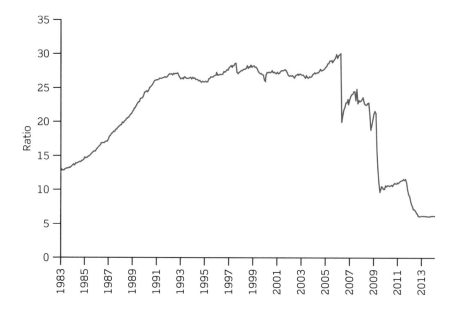

Figure 5.5 Ratio of broad money to narrow money (including reserve balances).
Note: (i) Numerator is M4; Denominator is M0 up to April 2006 and reserves plus notes and coins from May 2006; (ii) data are seasonally adjusted except for reserves.
Source: Based on series LPMAUYN (M4), LPMAVAE (M0) LPMBL22 (reserves) and LPMAVAB (notes and coins) from *Statistical Interactive Database*, Bank of England (data published 2 and 3 April 2013).

The demand for money

Money is one way in which economic agents can hold their wealth. An important reason for holding some wealth in this liquid form is the ability to engage in transactions. This is the **transactions demand for money**. The amount of money balances held for transactions will largely depend on the amount of output (real GDP) of the country and the prices of goods and services. The greater the level of economic activity and the higher the prices are, the greater the money balances held.

Another motive for holding money is uncertainty and unforeseen circumstances. This is the **precautionary demand for money**. Greater economic uncertainty will, all other things being equal, increase the demand for money balances.

A third commonly identified motive for holding money is the **speculative demand for money**. This recognises that there are alternative ways in which to hold wealth. We could hold it, for instance, in more illiquid financial assets or in goods and services, including housing. The speculative demand for money will be affected both by the current rates of return on the alternative methods of holding wealth and by our expectations of future rates of return. The demand for money will tend to be greater the lower the returns on alternative forms of holding wealth and will increase if these returns are expected to fall.

Key definitions

Transactions demand for money

The motivation to hold wealth as money in order to engage in transactions.

Precautionary demand for money

The motivation to hold money due to uncertainty and unforeseen circumstances.

Speculative demand for money

The motivation to hold money because of the current or expected return on alternative forms of holding wealth.

Recap

By engaging in a process of credit creation, banks can cause the money supply to expand. This occurs as the spending caused by bank lending is deposited with banks. These deposits then become the funds for further lending and, in turn, even more deposits. The extent to which this process continues depends on several factors, including the liquidity ratio of banks and the demand of the non-bank private sector to hold its wealth in deposits with the banking sector.

Test yourself

Q1. How can banks, merely by changing their composition of assets, cause the balance sheet to expand?

Q2. What impact does the liquidity ratio have on the extent of credit creation?

The central bank

The role of the central bank

The UK's central bank is the Bank of England. Its first core objective is to carry out monetary policy. Since 1997, the Bank of England has had independence over monetary policy. Each month the Bank of England's Monetary Policy Committee (MPC) sets the bank rate. The Bank of England looks to influence the structure of interest rates in the economy.

The second core objective of the Bank of England is financial stability. It oversees the activities of banks and other financial institutions and monitors the financial system. Following the financial crisis and the formation of the Coalition government in 2010, the Bank of England has acquired enhanced powers as the overseer and regulator of the financial system. First, the Financial Policy Committee (FPC) is responsible for maintaining financial stability by assessing the financial resilience of the financial system. Second, the Prudential Regulation Authority (PRA), a subsidiary of the Bank of England, undertakes the prudential regulation of individual firms. The Financial Conduct Authority (FCA) is responsible for consumer protection and the regulation of markets for financial services. It is an independent body accountable to the Treasury.

In addition to operating monetary policy and 'overseeing' the UK financial system, other roles for the Bank of England include the following:

- It provides liquidity to the banking system to ensure financial stability.
- It is the sole issuer of banknotes in England and Wales (in Scotland and Northern Ireland, retail banks issue banknotes).
- It acts as a banker to the government. The government's general bank account is known as The Consolidated Fund.
- It acts as the banker for banks. Commercial banks hold reserve balances for settlement of accounts between banks and as a source of liquidity.
- It acts as a banker to overseas central banks. The Bank of England holds deposits of British pounds made by the authorities of other countries.

Conduct of UK monetary policy

The Bank of England is charged with meeting the government's annual CPI (Consumer Price Index) inflation rate target of 2 per cent plus or minus 1 per cent. Each month the MPC meets to decide the bank rate. The Bank of England will engage in short-term lending to financial institutions at this interest rate. In doing so, it hopes to affect other interest rates in the economy and, thereby, affect the level of aggregate demand. For example, in looking to reduce the rate of inflation it will raise the bank rate, which, in turn, will cause other interest rates, such as mortgage rates, to rise. The intention is that higher interest rates will, in due course, reduce aggregate demand and reduce expectations of inflation.

The means through which interest rate changes affect the rate of inflation is an example of what economists call a **transmission mechanism**. A transmission mechanism describes how policy changes are expected to affect a policy target, such as inflation. There can often be several channels through which policy changes work. For example, a higher interest rate makes saving more attractive and borrowing more expensive, thereby helping to reduce aggregate demand. Higher interest rates also affect cash flows by increasing the income from saving but increasing the interest payments on loans, such as on residential mortgages. The effect of the latter is typically observed to be stronger, so again the net effect on aggregate demand is negative.[1]

The reserve account balances of commercial banks at the Bank of England are a crucial part of the UK's monetary framework. As well as a means of settling payments between banks, reserve accounts also allow banks to manage their level of liquidity. Financial institutions can reduce (increase) their reserves to reduce (increase) their liquidity ratio.

Key definition

Transmission mechanism
The means by which policy changes affect policy targets, such as an inflation rate target.

✳ Assessment advice

In looking to affect inflation, the Bank of England manipulates interest rates. In turn, this should affect aggregate demand. However, as we shall see later (Chapter 6), economists distinguish between inflation originating from rising aggregate demand (demand-pull inflation) and inflation originating from rising costs of production (cost-push inflation). A problem for the Bank of England in the late 2000s and again in the early 2010s was inflationary pressures accompanied by weak growth. An important source of this inflationary pressure was global commodity prices (e.g. fuel, foodstuffs and metals).

A bank's demand for reserves will depend on economic conditions and the general pattern of payment flows. Payment flows can be affected by the flows of government spending, taxation receipts and borrowing. Assume that on a given day tax payments made by banks' customers are greater than the flows of government expenditure they receive. Customers will be drawing on their bank accounts and, in turn, there will be a corresponding transfer of funds from the banks' reserve accounts at the Bank of England to the government's account. A similar process occurs when government issues debt instruments, such as gilts, to 'plug the gap' between its spending and its taxation.

---

1 For more information on the transmission mechanism of monetary policy visit **www.bankofengland.co.uk/monetarypolicy/Pages/how.aspx**.

The Bank of England forecasts the *aggregate* amount of reserves that the banking system needs in order to keep short-term rates of interest at which banks borrow from and lend to each other close to the bank rate. It does this through **open-market operations** (OMOs). OMOs are the sale or purchase by the Bank of England of government debt securities on the open market.

Key definition

Open-market operations (OMOs)
The sale or purchase by the central bank of government debt instruments on the open market.

Assume that the Bank of England forecasts that it needs to provide the banking system with additional reserves to prevent upward pressure on interbank interest rates. The Bank of England will provide banks with funds through short-term repo lending, usually over a week, charged at the bank rate (policy rate). This means that the Bank of England provides reserves secured against eligible collateral, such as government bonds.

In addition to managing the aggregate amount of reserves, the Bank of England also allows individual commercial banks to deposit or borrow reserves through its **operational standing facilities**. Banks can deposit reserves at the deposit facility rate if they have an excess of reserves. Alternatively, they can borrow reserves directly from the Bank of England through an overnight repo at the lending facility rate if they are short of reserves. The deposit rate is set below the bank rate and the borrowing rate is set above the bank rate.

From May 2006 to March 2009, commercial banks agreed with the Bank of England an *average* amount of overnight reserve balances they would hold over the period between MPC meetings. Reserves within plus or minus 1 per cent of the target were then remunerated at the bank rate. Any excess reserves had to be moved to the deposit facility and were remunerated at 100 basis points (1 percentage point) below the base rate. On the other hand, any overnight borrowing would be charged at 100 basis points above the base rate. This process is known as **reserve averaging**.

The operational standing facilities provide those banks with an excess or surplus of reserves an incentive to trade reserves with other banks if interbank rates are more favourable. Therefore, banks would prefer to borrow (deposit) reserves at a lower (higher) interest rate from (with) other banks rather than using the operational standing facilities at the Bank of England. This should then establish a 'corridor' for interbank rates between the lending and deposit rates at the Bank of England.

Key definitions

Operational standing facilities

Central bank facilities by which individual banks can deposit reserves or borrow reserves.

Reserve averaging

The process whereby individual banks manage their average level of overnight reserves between MPC meetings using the Bank of England's operational standing facilities and/or the interbank market.

Recap

In conducting monetary policy, the Bank of England attempts to ensure that short-term interest rates are close to the bank rate. In normal times, it uses short-term open-market operations (OMOs) to supply an aggregate amount of reserves, agrees an average overnight reserve target with individual banks and provides operational standing facilities where banks can deposit or borrow reserves. The standing facility rates are set to provide banks with an incentive to trade reserves with each other.

Test yourself

Q1. Why do the standing facility deposit and lending rates give banks an incentive to trade reserves with each other?

Q2. What do you understand by open-market operations? How can OMOs be used by the Bank of England to increase the aggregate amount of reserves?

UK monetary policy and the financial crisis

The financial crisis of the late 2000s meant that it became more difficult for the Bank of England to meet simultaneously its two core objectives of conducting monetary policy and ensuring financial stability. Consequently, the monetary policy framework evolved. For instance, in October 2008 the Bank of England's penalty rates for using its deposit and borrowing operational facilities were reduced from plus or minus 100 basis points around the bank rate to plus or minus 25 basis points.

However, a major factor in the evolution of the monetary framework occurred in March 2009 when the Bank of England began its programme of

quantitative easing. This involved the Bank of England purchasing assets, mainly government debt instruments, from financial institutions. The effect of this was to supply banks with reserves. The hope was that this would help banks to create credit and so boost aggregate demand. The Bank of England believed that without doing so it would 'undershoot' its inflation rate target because of the weakness of aggregate demand.

With quantitative easing providing large amounts of reserves to the banking system, the Bank of England suspended reserve averaging and thereby the system of banks voluntarily setting their own reserve targets. Furthermore, *all* reserves were now to be remunerated at the official bank rate. The bank rate fell to 0.5 per cent in March 2009. Since banks were now having reserves remunerated at the bank rate, they no longer needed to deposit reserves with the operational standing facility. The operational standing deposit facility rate was set at zero while the rate charged on the operational standing lending facility became 0.75 per cent (bank rate of 0.5 per cent plus 0.25 per cent).

Because of the financial crisis, the Bank of England introduced a further mechanism by which banks can obtain liquid funds. It is known as the **Discount Window Facility** (DWF). With the DWF, banks can borrow government bonds (gilts) for 30 or 364 days against a wide range of collateral. They pay a fee to do so. Gilts are long-term government debt instruments used by government as a means of financing its borrowing. Gilts can be used in repo operations (see above) as a means of securing liquidity.

Despite recent changes, banks' reserve accounts and the operational standing facility remain central to the operation of UK monetary policy.

Key definitions

Quantitative easing

Large-scale open-market operations to increase the supply of money.

Discount Window Facility

A means by which banks and building societies can borrow gilts (government bonds) from the Bank of England for 30 or 364 days against a wide range of collateral.

Chapter summary – pulling it all together

By the end of this chapter you should be able to:

	Confident ✓	Not confident?
Detail the types of financial institutions		Revise pages 109–110
Detail the role of financial institutions		Revise pages 110–113
Explain the types of financial instruments provided by banks and building societies		Revise pages 113–115
Analyse what is recorded on the balance sheet of banks and building societies		Revise pages 116–117
Describe how the aggregate balance sheet of UK banks and building societies has evolved		Revise pages 117–120
Detail the functions of money		Revise pages 120–121
Explain what is meant by 'narrow' and 'broad' measures of the money supply		Revise pages 121–123
Describe the process of credit creation		Revise pages 123–126
Explain the role of the bank of England		Revise pages 127–128
Analyse how the Bank of England conducts monetary policy		Revise pages 128–131
Discuss how UK monetary policy has evolved following the financial crisis		Revise pages 131–132

Now try the assessment question at the start of this chapter, using the answer guidelines below.

Answer guidelines

✳ Assessment question

What financial instruments are recorded on the aggregate balance sheet of banks and building societies? What role do these financial instruments play in the Bank of England's conduct of monetary policy?

Approaching the question

The question provides you with the opportunity to demonstrate an awareness of the variety of financial instruments that form the assets and liabilities of financial institutions. It therefore provides an opportunity to show your awareness of both the size and composition of the banking sector's aggregate balance sheet. Finally, the question is asking for both a description of the operations of monetary policy and an economic analysis of these operations. In other words, what can economic thinking bring to our understanding of how monetary policy is undertaken?

Important points to include

- **Definition of the concept of a financial instrument.** Explain what is meant by a financial instrument and how the resulting financial claims result in asset or liability for banks and building societies.

- **The variety of financial instruments.** This is your opportunity to show not only your awareness but also your understanding of the variety of financial instruments.

- **Aggregate balance sheet.** You should consider presenting a representation of the aggregate balance sheet. This does not need to contain monetary values as in Table 5.1. You can use this to help explore the financial instruments.

- **Overview of the objectives of UK monetary policy.** Describe how the Bank of England is charged with meeting an inflation rate target set by government. Go on to describe how it agrees monthly on the bank rate and then conducts monetary policy so that short-term interest rates approach the bank rate. The aim is to affect aggregate demand and inflationary expectations.

- **Operational details of UK monetary policy.** Explain the key ingredients of the UK's monetary framework: the use of open-market operations by the Bank of England to supply an aggregate amount of reserves, agreement with commercial banks on reserve targets and the provision of operational standing facilities.

Make your answer stand out

- Try to avoid simply *listing* the financial instruments. Explore what functions these instruments play and what economic impact they can have. For instance, under 'advances' we have financial instruments providing longer-term credit facilities to households and businesses.

- Although it is not essential to remember the exact monetary values of the assets and liabilities that comprise the balance sheets, explore their relative importance, significance and impact on the overall balance sheet.

- Use economic analysis to help explore the *transmission mechanism* through which monetary policy aims to meet the government's inflation rate target.

- Use economic analysis to explain *how* the UK's monetary framework is expected to deliver short-term interest rates approaching the bank rate.

- Better answers will explore the ways in which the monetary framework has evolved following the financial crisis.

Read to impress

Here are some books, articles and other sources that you can use to develop your answers on the topic area.

Books

Griffiths, A. and Wall, S. (2011) *Economics for Business and Management*, 3rd edition, Chapter 10, 'Government policies: instruments and objectives'. Harlow, UK: Pearson Education.

Parkin, M., Powell, M. and Matthews, K. (2012) *Essential Economics*, European edition, Chapter 12, 'Financial markets'. Harlow, UK: Pearson Education.

Parkin, M., Powell, M. and Matthews, K. (2012) *Essential Economics*, European edition, Chapter 13, 'Money and banking'. Harlow, UK: Pearson Education.

Sloman, J. and Garratt, D. (2013) *Essentials of Economics*, 6th edition, Chapter 10, 'Banking, money and interest rates'. Harlow, UK: Pearson Education.

Articles

Butt, N., Domit, S., McLeay, M., Thomas, R. and Kirkham, L. (2012) What can the money data tell us about the impact of QE? *Bank of England Quarterly Bulletin*, Q4: 321–31 (www.bankofengland.co.uk/publications/Documents/quarterlybulletin/qb120402.pdf).

Clews, R., Salmon, C. and Weeken, O. (2010) The Bank's money market framework. *Bank of England Quarterly Bulletin*, Q4: 292–301 (www.bankofengland.co.uk/publications/Documents/quarterlybulletin/qb100404.pdf).

Davies, R., Richardson, P., Katinaite, V. and Manning, M. (2011) The United Kingdom's quantitative easing policy: design, operation and impact. *Bank of England Quarterly Bulletin*, Q4: 321–332. (www.bankofengland.co.uk/publications/Documents/quarterlybulletin/qb100407.pdf).

Joyce, M., Tong, M. and Woods, R. (2011) The United Kingdom's quantitative easing policy: design, operation and impact. *Bank of England Quarterly Bulletin*, Q3: 200–12 (www.bankofengland.co.uk/publications/Documents/quarterlybulletin/qb110301.pdf).

Periodicals and newspapers

The Bank of England's *Inflation Report* contains a readable overview of recent developments in the national economy including the financial system.

The Bank of England's *Financial Stability Report* is a twice-yearly assessment of the outlook for the stability and resilience of the financial sector.

BBC News (2012) 'Bank reforms should be tougher', Banking Commission says. 21 December.

Financial Times (2012) Quantitative easing: older than you think. Claire Jones, 7 August.

Financial Times (2012) Northern Rock exposed regulatory failings. Brooke Masters, 12 September.

Financial Times (2012) Business cash holdings pick up. Daniel Pimlott, 29 October.

Financial Times (2012) Infrastructure hopes hit by City stand-off. Gill Plimmer, Patrick Jenkins and Jim Pickard, 18 November.

Financial Times (2012) Credit Suisse splits investment banking. Paul J Davies, 20 November.

Financial Times (2012) BOJ adds Y10tn to easing programme. Michiyo Nakamoto, 20 December.

Financial Times (2012) Banking review calls for stricter reforms. Patrick Jenkins and George Parker, 21 December.

Financial Times (2013) Banks, here's your new liquidity regime. Now stop blaming us. Love, Basel. Kate Mackenzie, 7 January.

Companion website

Go to the companion website at **www.pearsoned.co.uk/econexpress** to find more revision support online for this topic area.

Notes

Notes

6 Unemployment and inflation

Topic map

- Revision checklist
- Assessment question

Introduction

Unemployment
- Measures of unemployment
- Equilibrium and disequilibrium unemployment
- Types of equilibrium unemployment
- Types of disequilibrium unemployment

Unemployment and inflation

Inflation
- Costs of inflation
- Causes of inflation

Chapter summary
- Test yourself
- Answer guidelines
- Read to impress

Expectations-augmented Phillips curve

Phillips curve
- The Phillips curve mechanism

- Expectations and the short-run Phillips curve
- The accelerationist theory
- Rational expectations and wage-setting
- Central bank independence

A printable version of this topic map is available from **www.pearsoned.co.uk/econexpress**

Introduction

Figure 6.1 allows us to track *rates* of unemployment and price inflation in the UK since the early 1960s. The unemployment rate is the *percentage* of the labour force (the sum of those employed or unemployed) that are unemployed. The annual rate of inflation shown here is the annual percentage increase in the GDP deflator (the economy's average price level). We can see considerable variations in both macroeconomic indicators.

Consider first the variations in the unemployment rate. Since 1961, the average rate of unemployment has been close to 6 per cent. However, during this period, the unemployment rate was as low as 1.1 per cent in 1966, but as high as 11.2 per cent in 1985 and again in 1986. The rate of unemployment was higher across the 1980s than it had been in the 1970s and, in turn, higher than it had been in the 1960s. The rate of unemployment then began falling after the early 1990s, before rising at the end of the 2000s because of the economic downturn following the financial crisis.

We also observe variability in the rate of inflation. The average annual rate of increase in the GDP deflator since 1961 is around 6 per cent. However, the rate of inflation in 1975 was 27 per cent compared with only 0.7 per cent in 1999. Figure 6.1 also shows that the variability in the rate of inflation tends

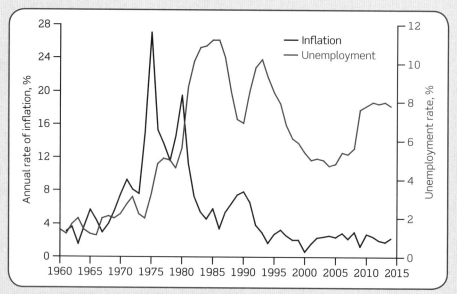

Figure 6.1 UK rates of inflation and unemployment.

Note: (i) unemployment rate is unemployed persons as a share of the total civilian labour force; (ii) inflation rate is the annual percentage change in the GDP deflator; (iii) data from 2012 based on forecasts.

Source: Based on data from *AMECO database*, DG ECFIN, European Commission.

to be greatest when the rate of inflation is at its highest. More recently, the spread of inflation rates has been lower. Since 1997, the rate of inflation has been just less than half the longer-term average. As we saw previously (Chapter 5), this period has seen the Bank of England set interest rates to meet a government-set inflation rate target.

 Assessment advice

Awareness of patterns and trends in unemployment and inflation data can help to contextualise your answer to any assessment based on these issues. The data can also provide depth to your analysis.

In this chapter, we look at unemployment and inflation in more detail, focusing on the possible determinants of both. We then move on to consider the relationship between the two. In doing so, we look at the well-known Phillips curve, which is based on an observed empirical relationship in the UK from 1861 to 1957 between rates of (wage) inflation and unemployment. We consider whether policy-makers can exploit any trade-off between inflation and unemployment. As we shall see, this issue divides economists.

We conclude by considering how economists' understanding of the relationship between unemployment and inflation has resulted in many central banks, such as the Bank of England, being granted some form of independence in their conduct of monetary policy.

 Revision checklist

What you need to know:
- ❑ How we measure unemployment.
- ❑ The different types of unemployment.
- ❑ Potential causes of unemployment.
- ❑ Costs of inflation.
- ❑ Causes of inflation.
- ❑ The economics behind the 'simple' Phillips curve.
- ❑ The expectations-augmented Phillips curve and the accelerationist hypothesis.
- ❑ The role of expectations and wage-setting behaviour in affecting the inflation–unemployment trade-off.
- ❑ How independent central banks can reduce inflation bias.

Assessment question

Can you answer this essay-type question? Guidelines on answering the question are presented at the end of this chapter.

Does the Phillips curve relationship demonstrate that policy-makers can trade off lower unemployment against higher inflation?

Unemployment

Measures of unemployment

The internationally recognised measure of unemployment is the **standardised unemployment rate**. Under this measure, the unemployed are those people of working age who are without work, available to start work within two weeks and actively seeking employment or waiting to take up an appointment. The standardised unemployment rate is calculated as the number of unemployed people as a percentage of the **labour force**, that is those employed plus those unemployed. The standardised unemployment rate for the UK since 1961 is shown in Figure 6.1.

Countries also publish administrative unemployment figures. In the UK, this is referred to as the **claimant count** and is based on those entitled to 'Jobseeker's Allowance'. Administrative measures are more difficult to compare over time or between countries. This is because entitlements to unemployment-related benefits vary over time and between countries. International and historical comparisons, therefore, use standardised unemployment rates.

The level or stock of unemployed people is affected by the flows into and out of unemployment. During any period there will be a flow of people *into* unemployment. These are flows of people out of jobs, such as those made redundant, as well as people from outside the labour force, such as school leavers, seeking employment. However, during any period there will be flows *out of* unemployment. These include people entering employment or people leaving the labour force. When the flows out of unemployment are greater than the flows into unemployment the number of people unemployed will fall. The rate of these flows will also affect the *duration* of unemployment. The more quickly people move in and out of unemployment, the shorter will be the average duration of unemployment.

 Assessment advice

The distinction between stocks and flows is a crucial one in economics. In the current context, the stock of unemployed people rises or falls depending on the *flows* into unemployment and out of unemployment.

Standardised unemployment rate

The percentage of the workforce of working age without work who are available for work and are actively seeking employment.

Labour force

People who are economically active and either in employment or unemployed.

Claimant count

An administrative measure of unemployment based on those entitled to the 'Jobseeker's Allowance'.

Equilibrium and disequilibrium unemployment

Earlier, we made the distinction between two types of unemployment: disequilibrium and equilibrium unemployment (see Chapter 1). **Disequilibrium unemployment** occurs when the real wage rate is above the equilibrium rate. **Equilibrium unemployment** occurs because the number of people willing and able to accept jobs is less than the number of people in the workforce.

Disequilibrium unemployment

Unemployment that results from real wages being above their equilibrium level.

Equilibrium unemployment

The difference between those willing to take employment at current wage rates and those actually able to.

To deepen our understanding of disequilibrium and equilibrium unemployment we can construct a simple model of the aggregate labour market as shown in Figure 6.2. On the vertical axis is the average real wage rate. This is found by 'deflating' the average nominal (actual) wage rate by a measure of consumer prices. In other words, we adjust the actual wage rate for the level of consumer prices so that the average real wage rate captures the purchasing power of workers' wages.

First, consider the *aggregate labour demand curve* (L_D). It is drawn as downward sloping because, as the real wage rate falls, it becomes more profitable for firms to hire additional workers, all other things remaining equal.

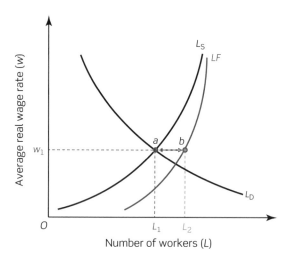

Figure 6.2 Aggregate labour market.

Second, consider *the labour force curve* (LF). This plots the size of the labour force against the average real wage rate. We would expect the size of the labour force to rise with the real wage rate since people not previously in the labour force would choose to become economically active. However, the extent to which the size of the labour force is responsive to changes in the real wage rate is uncertain. We would also expect there to be, at least in the short term, an upper limit to the size of the labour force. The labour force curve is typically depicted as becoming progressively less responsive to real wage increases.

Third, consider the *aggregate labour supply curve* (L_s). It lies to the left of the labour force curve because it shows the number of those in the labour force who are willing and able to *accept* work at each real wage rate. It is drawn as upward sloping because the higher the real wage rate, the greater the number of people in the labour force who are willing to accept jobs. Therefore, people previously unemployed become more willing to take work rather than continuing to search for other opportunities.

Equilibrium in the aggregate labour market occurs at average real wage rate w_1 with L_1 workers employed. At real wage rate w_1 aggregate labour demand equals aggregate labour supply. However, not everybody in the labour force is in employment at this real wage. The horizontal distance $b - a$ captures the difference at real wage w_1 between the total number in the labour force (L_2) and the number of workers willing to accept employment (L_1). Therefore, at w_1, equilibrium unemployment is $L_2 - L_1$.

Assume now that the real wage rate is above the equilibrium real wage rate w_1, at say w_2 as shown in Figure 6.3. We now have excess supply as depicted by the horizontal distance $d - c$. This is disequilibrium employment. However,

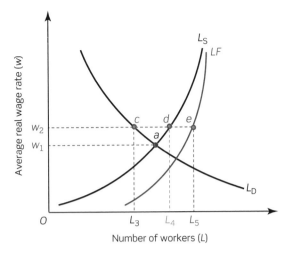

Figure 6.3 Aggregate labour market.

at real wage rate w_2 total unemployment is $e - c$ ($L_5 - L_3$). Of this, $d - c$ ($L_4 - L_3$) is disequilibrium unemployment and $e - d$ ($L_5 - L_4$) is equilibrium unemployment.

Types of equilibrium unemployment

We have seen that equilibrium unemployment occurs when at the current real wage the size of the labour force exceeds the number of people willing and able to take a job. It is important for policy-makers to be able to distinguish between types of equilibrium unemployment. Each will require different policy measures. The following are types of equilibrium unemployment:

- **Frictional unemployment.** This is unemployment resulting from employers searching for prospective workers and employees searching for prospective employers. Therefore, frictional unemployment is also known as *search unemployment*. Frictions in the labour market, such as imperfect information or disincentives to search, mean that it takes longer or becomes more difficult to match prospective employers and employees. For instance, prospective workers may hold out for a better-paid job or be unaware of the available opportunities. Similarly, firms may hold back from hiring workers or advertising vacancies, wrongly believing that suitable candidates are unavailable.

- **Structural unemployment.** This occurs because of a mismatch in the skills of potential workers and those sought by employers or a mismatch between the location of prospective workers and employers. Consequently, it also known as *mismatch unemployment*. It can result from structural changes in the economy. For example, the UK has experienced a marked change in its industrial composition with a declining share of output from

145

manufacturing and an increasing share from services. Structural changes also occur with changes in production methods, such as those that result from technological progress. Structural unemployment can result, too, from impediments that make it difficult for people to move between geographical locations.

● *Seasonal unemployment.* This occurs with fluctuations in the demand for labour across the seasons. Examples include employment in tourism and agriculture.

Key definitions

Frictional (search) unemployment

Frictions in the labour market, such as imperfect information, which cause unemployment as workers search for employment and firms search for employees.

Structural (mismatch) unemployment

Unemployment that results from a mismatch between the skills of potential workers and those demanded by employers or from a mismatch between the location of potential workers and employers.

Types of disequilibrium unemployment

There are two principal types of disequilibrium unemployment:

● **Real wage unemployment.** This occurs when the current real wage rate is above the equilibrium real wage rate. It could be the result of government setting the national minimum wage too high. Alternatively, it could result from the power of those in employment, sometimes referred to as 'insiders', driving wages above market clearing at the expense of those seeking employment, namely 'outsiders'. This results in an excess supply of labour and hence disequilibrium unemployment (see Figure 6.3).

● **Demand-deficient unemployment.** This results from fluctuations in economic growth. Consider Figure 6.4. Assume initially that the aggregate labour market is in equilibrium at point *a* with the aggregate demand for labour matched by the aggregate supply of labour. Therefore, at this point there is no disequilibrium unemployment, only equilibrium unemployment ($b-a$). Assume now that as a result of an economic slowdown the aggregate labour demand curve shifts leftwards from L_{D_1} to L_{D_2}, but that real wages are 'sticky' and remain at w_1. The result is disequilibrium unemployment equivalent to the horizontal distance $a-f$, and so to L_1-L_3 workers.

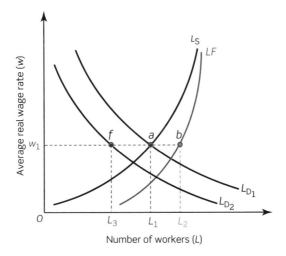

Figure 6.4 Demand-deficient unemployment.

 Key definitions

Real wage unemployment
Unemployment that occurs because the current real wage rate is above the equilibrium real wage rate, causing an excess supply of labour.

Demand-deficient unemployment
Unemployment that results from a fall in aggregate demand without a corresponding fall in the real wage rate.

✳ Assessment advice

In describing the types of equilibrium and disequilibrium unemployment, reflect on the different types of *policy prescriptions* needed to reduce each.

Recap

We can distinguish between equilibrium and disequilibrium unemployment. Equilibrium unemployment occurs when, at the current wage rate, the number willing and able to accept employment (labour supply) is less than the number of people in the labour force. Disequilibrium unemployment occurs when the current real wage rate is above the equilibrium wage rate.

Test yourself

Q1. Can an economy exhibit both equilibrium and disequilibrium unemployment?

Q2. Draw up a list of the types of policies that could be pursued to tackle equilibrium unemployment and then repeat the exercise for disequilibrium unemployment.

Inflation

Inflation refers to rising prices. The **annual rate of inflation** measures the annual percentage increase in prices. Perhaps the best-known measure of prices is the consumer price index (CPI) which tracks the cost of a broad range of consumer goods and services. A broader measure of prices tracks the cost of all domestically produced goods and services. This is the GDP deflator or, more simply, the economy's average price level. Figure 6.1 (on p. 140) shows the annual rates of change in the GDP deflator in the UK since 1961.

Key definitions

Inflation
A rise in the *level* of prices.

Annual rate of inflation
The percentage increase in the level of prices over a 12-month period.

Assessment advice

Take care to distinguish between increases in price *levels* and increases in the *rate* of price inflation. It is a very common mistake.

The costs of inflation

Three commonly identified 'costs' of inflation are:

- *Menu costs.* The costs to firms of having to change price labels and menus.
- *Redistribution.* Inflation erodes the purchasing power of those on fixed incomes or those whose income streams grow less quickly than prices. However, inflation erodes the real value of outstanding stocks of debt. If inflation results in nominal incomes increasing more quickly than the costs

to borrowers of servicing their debt (their capital and interest payments), the proportion of income devoted to debt repayments will decline.

- *Uncertainty.* Higher rates of inflation are often accompanied by greater *fluctuations* in the rate of inflation (see Figure 6.1). This makes it more difficult for firms to plan ahead, which can be a deterrent to investment. Investment is crucial to an economy's longer-term rate of growth.

Causes of inflation

Economists commonly distinguish between two types of inflation: demand-pull inflation and cost-push inflation. We can illustrate these using the *AD–AS* model that we introduced earlier (see Chapter 3).

Demand-pull inflation is inflation that originates from increases in aggregate demand. A single increase in aggregate demand (a demand 'shock'), such as from AD_1 to AD_2 in Figure 6.5, will cause a one-off rise in the GDP deflator. The mainstream view of the short-run *AS* curve is that it becomes increasingly steeper as the economy reaches its full-capacity output. Therefore, the degree to which the price level rises for a given increase in aggregate demand will depend on the current level of output. The higher the current level of output relative to full-capacity output, the larger the increase in the GDP deflator.

Continuing increases in aggregate demand will cause inflation to persist. The rate of inflation will then depend on the magnitude of the increases in aggregate demand.

> ### Key definition
>
> **Demand-pull inflation**
> Inflation caused by persistent increases in aggregate demand.

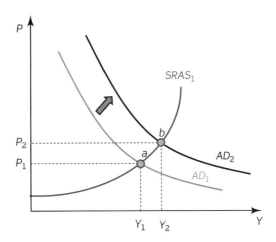

Figure 6.5 Demand-pull inflation.

Demand-pull inflation is often associated with a booming economy. This implies that the rate of economic growth is positively related to the rate of inflation. The reality is often more complex than this because of other causes of inflation.

Cost-push inflation is inflation that originates from increases in input prices, independently of changes in aggregate demand. The effect of higher input prices is to shift the short-run aggregate supply leftwards (see Chapter 3). Again, we can distinguish between one-off shifts in aggregate supply (a supply 'shock') and continual upward shifts in aggregate supply.

Figure 6.6 shows the effect of an increase in input prices. The result is a higher GDP deflator (P_1 to P_2) and a reduction in real GDP (Y_1 to Y_2). Persistent cost-push inflation is caused by the aggregate supply curve continually moving upwards. The rate of cost-push inflation then depends on the rate at which the AS curve is moving upwards.

> **Key definition**
>
> **Cost-push inflation**
> Inflation arising from persistent increases in the costs of production.

Frequently, demand-pull and cost-push inflation occur together. For example, the recent rapid economic development of countries such as China, India and Brazil has helped fuel the global demand for commodities used in production, including oil and metals. Since the mid-2000s, we have had periodic bursts of high rates of global commodity price inflation. During 2010 and 2011, for instance, commodity price inflation picked up sharply. This drove up input costs. By September 2011, the UK's annual CPI inflation rate was running at 5.2 per cent. This meant that despite weak economic growth in the UK,

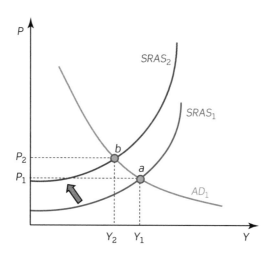

Figure 6.6 Cost-push inflation.

inflation was significantly above the Bank of England's inflation rate target of 2 per cent plus or minus 1 per cent.

Expectations of inflation also have a significant effect on actual inflation rates. Economic agents are likely to form expectations of inflation when entering into contractual negotiations over prices. For example, workers, when negotiating with employers over wages, will form expectations of inflation to maintain their spending power. In other words, they will want to maintain the *real* value of their income by ensuring that nominal wage increases at least match consumer price increases. Therefore, the higher the expected rate of inflation, the larger the increase in input prices and, in turn, the larger the increase in output prices.

Recap

It is customary to distinguish between inflation that originates from increases in aggregate demand (demand-pull inflation) and inflation that originates from decreases in aggregate supply (cost-push inflation). However, cost-push and demand-pull inflation frequently occur together.

Test yourself

Q1. Distinguish between an increase in prices and an increase in the rate of price inflation.

Q2. If the rate of inflation rises because workers raise their inflationary expectations, has the economy experienced demand-pull or cost-push inflation?

The Phillips curve

One of the most well-known economic relationships is the **Phillips curve**. In analysing the empirical relationship between wage inflation and unemployment in the UK between 1861 and 1957, A.W. Phillips found a non-linear, *negative* relationship. Wages are the most significant cost for most businesses so it has become customary to depict the Phillips curve as the relationship between price inflation and unemployment. Figure 6.7 illustrates the Phillips curve.

Key definition

Phillips curve

A curve showing the relationship between price inflation and unemployment. The original Phillips curve captured the empirical relationship between wage inflation and unemployment in the UK between 1861 and 1957.

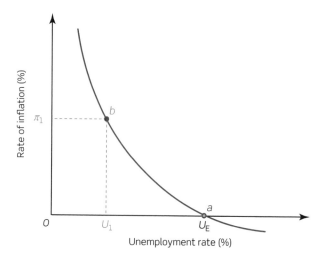

Figure 6.7 The Phillips curve.

> ### ✳ Assessment advice
>
> As with any diagram in macroeconomics, make sure that you draw your Phillips curve diagrams clearly, label them fully and, importantly, integrate them into the text of your answer.

The Phillips curve seemed to offer policy-makers a menu of inflation and unemployment choices. If they wanted to reduce unemployment, they needed to increase real aggregate demand, albeit at the cost of a higher rate of inflation. Therefore, changes in demand cause movements *along* the Phillips curve. In contrast, non-demand factors affect the *position* of the Phillips curve. For example, greater structural and frictional unemployment would result in the curve shifting rightwards. There would be a higher rate of unemployment and at any particular rate of inflation.

Now consider the case where the economy is currently at point *a* in Figure 6.7. At this point, the rate of inflation (π) is zero, while the unemployment rate is the equilibrium rate of unemployment (U_E) at which aggregate labour demand equals aggregate labour supply. If we revisit Figure 6.2 (page 144), the equilibrium rate of unemployment at the equilibrium real wage is $(L_2 - L_1)/L_2$.

Assume that policy-makers are looking to reduce the rate of unemployment below the equilibrium rate. To do so would require the policy-makers to accept a non-zero rate of inflation in return for a lower unemployment rate.

The Phillips curve mechanism

To understand how this trade-off might arise we revisit the *AD–AS* frame-work. In Figure 6.8 the economy is initially at the potential level of output, Y_1, which corresponds with the equilibrium rate of unemployment at point *a* in Figure 6.7. Assume that the government increases aggregate demand from AD_1 to AD_2 by increasing its spending. Since the economy's short-run *AS* curve is upwards sloping because the marginal cost of additional output is assumed to increase as output rises (see Chapter 3), both the level of output and the GDP deflator increase. Output increases to Y_2 and the GDP deflator to P_2.

The extent to which the GDP deflator rises depends on the extent to which output rises above potential output. This creates excess demand and, hence, a positive output gap (see Chapter 3). The larger the increase in aggregate demand relative to potential output, the higher the resulting rate of inflation. This explains why the Phillips curve is bowed (convex) to the origin.

This, however, is not the end of the story. Assume now that the increase in output prices causes the suppliers of inputs, including workers, to negotiate higher prices. As input prices rise, the short-run *AS* curve moves upwards ($SRAS_1$ to $SRAS_2$), the GDP deflator rises and output falls. If the government wants to maintain output at Y_2 (above potential output Y_1) and, hence, unemployment below the equilibrium rate, it would need to be continually shifting the *AD* curve to the right. So long as the rightward shifts of the *AD* curve sufficiently outweigh leftward shifts of the *SRAS* curve, then output can be kept at Y_2 rather than Y_1. Therefore, the key to the Phillips curve mechanism is that increases in aggregate demand are not completely offset by increases in input prices, including wages. In other words, *real* aggregate demand increases.

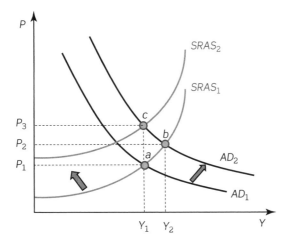

Figure 6.8 Illustrating the Phillips curve using *AD–AS*.

In attempting to keep output at Y_2 and, therefore, above potential output, policy-makers have to accept a continually rising GDP deflator. The rate of increase in the GDP deflator is the rate of inflation. The result is a corresponding point on the Phillips curve such as point b in Figure 6.7 with inflation rate π_1 and unemployment rate U_1.

✱ Assessment advice

It is important to demonstrate an understanding of the economic theory behind the idea that policy-makers might be able to choose a combination of inflation and unemployment on the Phillips curve. This will provide your answer with analytical depth.

Recap

The Phillips curve is based on empirical work examining the relationship between wage inflation and unemployment. Subsequent work by economists built theoretical underpinnings to explain how policy-makers could trade off unemployment below the equilibrium rate against a higher rate of inflation. It has been suggested that the Phillips curve trade-off arises out of increases in aggregate demand which are not absorbed by increases in input prices. Therefore, policy-makers are able to increase *real* aggregate demand.

Examples & evidence

The path of inflation and unemployment in the UK

The chart shows the rates of unemployment and inflation in each year in the UK since 1961. It shows a considerable spread of unemployment–inflation observations over this period. The period over which we observe a curve most similar to the original Phillips curve is the 1960s.

After the 1960s, the inflation–unemployment relationship in the UK appears to change. Inevitably, economists debate the reasons for this. Some point to *structural changes in the economy*, such as the decreasing share of manufacturing in national output. Others point to the need to take into account the *inflationary expectations* of workers (and other suppliers of inputs). They argue that inflation is determined not only by the economy's level of output relative to its potential output, but by inflationary expectations too.

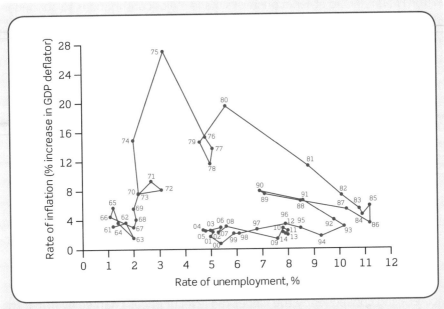

UK unemployment and inflation rates since 1961.

Note: data from 2012 based on forecasts.

Source: Based on data from *AMECO* database, DG ECFIN, European Commission.

The relationship changes again as we move through the 1990s. Now we can draw an almost horizontal line through the data. In 1997, the Bank of England was granted the authority to determine the bank rate (see Chapter 5). In deciding on the bank rate, the Bank of England looks to meet an inflation rate target set by government.

Questions

1. Looking at the chart, see if you can draw possible Phillips curves that fit different historical periods.

2. What might explain the near-horizontal Phillips curve observed in more recent times?

Expectations-augmented Phillips curve

Expectations and the short-run Phillips curve

The extent to which policy-makers can trade off lower unemployment (unemployment below the equilibrium rate) against higher inflation is a keenly debated issue within macroeconomics. The Phillips curve trade-off as described above relies on output prices rising more rapidly than input prices. Consequently, the suppliers of inputs, including workers, play 'catch up' in trying to maintain the real value of their factor payments.

Milton Friedman and other economists made major contributions to our under-standing of the Phillips curve relationship in the late 1960s. They argued that this analysis failed to take into account the role played by people's *expecta-tions* of inflation. After all, why should workers continually allow an erosion of their real wages from rising prices following an expansion of aggregate demand?

The idea that workers (and other suppliers of inputs) incorporate expectations of future prices into their wage negotiations significantly affects the ability of policy-makers permanently to trade off lower unemployment for higher infla-tion. The mainstream view is that such a trade-off is only likely in the short term. The implication is that there exists a vertical long-run Phillips curve.

The incorporation of expectations into the Phillips curve relationship gives rise to the **expectations-augmented Phillips curve** (EAPC). There are now two elements to the Phillips curve. First, as with the 'simple' Phillips curve relation-ship, the lower the unemployment rate relative to the equilibrium rate, the higher the rate of inflation. Second, there is the expected rate of inflation. The higher the expected rate of inflation, the higher the wage demands of workers and consequently the higher the level of prices charged by firms. The result of the second element is that there is now a 'family' of Phillips curves rather than a single Phillips curve. Each Phillips curve is associated with a dif-ferent expected rate of inflation. The higher the expected rate of inflation, the vertically higher the Phillips curves.

Key definition

Expectations-augmented Phillips curve

A short-run Phillips curve whose vertical position depends on the expected rate of inflation.

Figure 6.9 illustrates the expectations-augmented Phillips curve. Each EAPC has an associated expected rate of inflation and the vertical distance at the equilibrium unemployment rate is the expected rate of inflation. Therefore, the expected inflation rate (π^e) along PC_1 is zero and that along PC_2 is π_1.

Recap

The expectations-augmented Phillips curve, as its name suggests, incorporates expectations of inflation into the Phillips curve relationship. In doing so, it produces a series of short-run Phillips curves whose vertical position depends on the expectations of inflation.

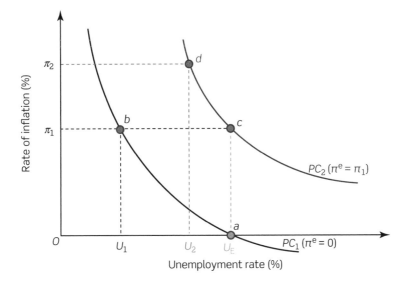

Figure 6.9 The expectations-augmented Phillips curve.

Test yourself

Q1. Why does the incorporation of expectations of inflation generate a 'family' of short-run Phillips curves?

Q2. Does a change in the expected rate of inflation cause a move along a Phillips curve or a movement of the Phillips curve?

The accelerationist theory

We now consider how the incorporation of expectations into the Phillips curve *might* affect the ability of policy-makers to trade off lower unemployment against a higher rate of inflation. To do so we need to make certain assumptions about how workers (and the suppliers of other inputs) set prices and how they form their inflationary expectations. For simplicity, assume that input prices are set at the beginning of each year for the year ahead. Assume too that workers expect the percentage change in prices over the coming year to be equal to the percentage change in prices that occurred in the previous year.

Assume that the economy is at point *a* in Figure 6.9, with unemployment at the equilibrium rate, a zero rate of inflation and also an expected inflation rate of zero. The government now expands aggregate demand in order to reduce unemployment below the equilibrium rate. The economy expands over the year, perhaps reaching a point like *b* with an unemployment rate of U_1 and an inflation rate of π_1. So far, the analysis is as before. However, here is the key difference: people at the start of the next year (year 2) now observe the inflation rate running at π_1. Consequently, they raise their inflationary expectations to π_1 and demand an equivalent nominal (actual) wage increase. The Phillips curve shifts up vertically by π_1.

Assume that in the second year aggregate demand increases in nominal (money) terms by the same percentage as the first year. The problem for policy-makers in trying to keep unemployment below the equilibrium rate is that, in the second year, the whole of the increase in the monetary value of the demands for firms' goods and services is absorbed by higher inputs costs. Therefore, despite *nominal* aggregate demand having risen, unemployment no longer falls and output no longer rises. In other words, *real* aggregate demand does not increase. The nominal increase in aggregate demand (a rightward shift of the *AD* curve) is entirely offset by the rise in wages and other input prices (a leftward shift of the *AS* curve).

 Assessment advice

The distinction between *nominal* aggregate demand and *real* aggregate demand is crucial to understanding the accelerationist hypothesis. If the proportionate increase in nominal aggregate demand is matched by an equivalent proportionate increase in prices then real aggregate demand is unchanged. The concepts of nominal and real are crucial in many areas of economics. We first came across them at the beginning of the text (see Chapter 1, pages 5–6). You might wish to revisit this if you are still a little unsure about them.

So, in the face of PC_2 and inflationary expectations of π_1, could the policy-maker in year 2 have done anything to keep unemployment below the equilibrium rate? The answer is that to do so it would need to ensure that the percentage increase in nominal aggregate demand is greater than the now higher expected rate of inflation, π_1. This means that the policy-maker needs to create *additional* inflation. For instance, assume that the policy-maker instigates an even larger rate of increase in nominal aggregate demand that moves the economy to point *d*. The actual inflation rate becomes π_2 and the unemployment rate U_2. To keep the unemployment rate at U_1 would require an even larger increase in nominal aggregate demand and a still higher inflation rate!

When the actual rate of inflation is greater than that expected by workers and other suppliers, the monetary increase in aggregate demand is not entirely offset by rising input costs. There is a *real* increase in aggregate demand.

However, even if the policy-makers did increase nominal demand at the faster rate in year 2 so as to keep unemployment below the equilibrium rate, they would still face the same issue at the start of year 3. This is because, with inflation during year 2 at π_2, workers will raise their inflationary expectations to π_2 at the start of year 3, and so the rate of increase in nominal aggregate demand in year 3 would need to rise still further. This pattern would be repeated year after year. Inflation must go on accelerating to keep unemployment below the equilibrium rate (and output above its potential level). Therefore, this theory of the Phillips curve is known as the **accelerationist theory**.

Key definition

Accelerationist theory

The theory that unemployment can only be kept below the equilibrium rate at the cost of accelerating inflation.

Recap

The accelerationist theory argues that to keep unemployment below the equilibrium rate requires an ever-increasing rate of growth in nominal aggregate demand. Otherwise, nominal increases in aggregate demand are absorbed by rising input costs, including wages, as the suppliers of inputs raise their inflationary expectations.

Test yourself

Q1. What is the distinction between nominal aggregate demand and real aggregate demand?

Q2. Explain why in the accelerationist theory the policy-maker needs to increase nominal aggregate demand at ever-faster rates in order to keep unemployment below the equilibrium rate.

Rational expectations and wage setting

The accelerationist theory of the Phillips curve can be thought of as a game involving policy-makers, firms and workers. It is an example of an application of what economists call **game theory**. Game theory allows us to analyse those situations where economic agents interact and where their choices affect others. It is important to understand how sensitive our conclusions are to the way in which the 'game' is played. In the context of the accelerationist model, we can alter the 'game' in two important ways. First, we can change the assumptions about how workers (and other suppliers of inputs) form their inflationary expectations. Second, we can change the assumptions about how wages and other input prices are determined.

> **Key definition**
>
> **Game theory**
> An analysis of strategic interactions among economic agents, such as those between workers, firms and policy-makers.

Consider first our assumptions about expectations. In the accelerationist model it is assumed that expectations of the inflation rate are based on past inflation. Backward-looking expectations are known as **adaptive expectations**. In the simplest case, as described above, this means that inflation expectations for the year ahead are based on last year's inflation rate. In contrast, rational expectations make use of the fullest possible information. Importantly, this includes information on the current state of the economy and on the policies pursued by government and the central bank.

The key point for our analysis of the inflation–unemployment trade-off is that with rational expectations economic agents do not make the same repeated error. In the accelerationist model, policy-makers can keep unemployment below the natural rate if they are prepared to accept accelerating inflation. This happens because economic agents are looking only at past inflation rates. They can be 'fooled' by the policy-maker if the policy-maker is willing to induce additional inflation by boosting aggregate demand.

With **rational expectations**, errors in predicting inflation are random. This means that if the policy-maker wants unemployment to be below the equilibrium rate, it needs to generate **surprise inflation**. In other words, for a given expectation of inflation (π^e) the policy-maker needs to induce additional inflation such that the expected inflation rate is *less* than the actual inflation rate. For example, assume the economy is at point c in Figure 6.9 and the policy-maker looks to increase the inflation rate to π_2. If, after taking into account expected government policies, workers forecast that the rate of inflation will be π_2 and are able to increase their wages accordingly, unemployment remains at U_E but with inflation at π_2. However, if their expected inflation rate is *less* than π_2 the unemployment rate will *fall*. The real value of aggregate demand increases. If the expected inflation rate was π_1 then the economy moves to point d.

> **Key definitions**
>
> **Adaptive expectations**
> Backward-looking expectations of a variable based on previous values.
>
> **Rational expectations**
> Expectations based on all available and relevant information such that economic agents' errors are random.

Surprise inflation

The situation where additional inflation, perhaps generated by policy-makers, causes the actual rate of inflation to be greater than expected.

The conclusion drawn is that by introducing rational expectations the ability of the policy-maker *repeatedly* to trade off lower unemployment for higher inflation is reduced.

Consider now the importance of our assumption about the determination of input prices. If workers and other suppliers of inputs are readily able to respond to surprise inflation then the trade-off is further weakened. At the extreme, if inputs prices are completely flexible then in conjunction with rational expectations the Phillips curve becomes vertical in both the short and long run. In reality, input prices are likely to exhibit some 'stickiness' because of contracts between the suppliers of inputs and their purchasers. Surprise inflation will therefore induce a short-term term trade-off between inflation and unemployment.

Recap

The extent to which policy-makers are able to trade off lower unemployment against higher inflation is argued to depend on both how economic agents form their expectations of inflation and how input prices, including wages, are determined.

Test yourself

Q1. In what ways do the assumptions of adaptive and rational expectations differ?

Q2. Does the assumption of rational expectations mean that the Phillips curve is vertical even in the short run?

Central bank independence and the Phillips curve

Many countries around the world have given their central bank some form of independence over monetary policy. In the case of the Bank of England this means this it has independence over the determination of interest rates, though its remit is an inflation rate target set by the Treasury (see Chapter 5).

Some of the theoretical justification for elected governments delegating control over monetary policy is derived from the game between policy-makers, firms and workers outlined above. If the trade-off between inflation and unemployment is, at best, short term then there may be grounds for depoliticising monetary policy and thereby removing the prospect that governments could use monetary policy in an attempt to enhance their election prospects.

If we look at Figure 6.9 then the optimal long-term position is point a, with unemployment at the equilibrium rate, U_E, and a rate of inflation of zero. However, if economic agents believe that policy-makers have an incentive to induce surprise inflation then this may prevent the economy from achieving this optimal long-term solution. To understand this, consider the scenario when the economy is currently at point a, wages are set at the start of the year, economic agents form rational expectations and an election is due later in the year.

Assume now that the government believes its chances of re-election improve if unemployment falls below the equilibrium rate. To bring this about, it needs to induce surprise inflation, say by reducing interest rates to stimulate aggregate demand, so that the actual rate of inflation exceeds the expected rate. This allows the *real* level of aggregate demand to increase.

The problem for the government is that the public know the government has the incentive to induce surprise inflation by loosening monetary policy. Consequently, the public, when forming expectations of inflation, use this information. The result is that the public raise their inflationary expectations and the economy moves to a vertically higher Phillips curve. However, the key point here is that economic agents raise their inflationary expectations by an amount sufficient for the government to be unwilling to generate even further inflation. This is because, in doing so with inflation already so high, it would no longer increase its re-election chances. This may mean raising inflationary expectations to π_1 so that the long-term position is c rather than a. The vertical distance c – a is known as **inflation bias**.

Key definition

Inflation bias

Excessive inflation resulting from workers and other suppliers of inputs maintaining high inflation rate expectations.

Inflation bias measures the degree to which the long-term inflation rate is above zero. Of course, it may be that economic agents need to raise their inflationary expectations even higher than π_1 to remove the government's incentive to induce surprise inflation. In delegating monetary policy to independent central bankers, the hope is to reduce the rate of inflation. This should be especially so where the remit of the central bank is defined solely in terms of an inflation rate target. Since May 1997, the Bank of England has been setting interest rates to meet an inflation rate target.

In the 'Examples & evidence' section above, we consider the path of inflation and unemployment in the UK since the early 1960s. There, we can see the effect of inflation rate targeting on the Phillips curve. The 'curve' has become more of a horizontal line.

Recap

If policy-makers are perceived to have an incentive to generate surprise inflation, workers will raise their expectations of inflation. Consequently, many countries have granted their central bank independence over monetary policy. In the UK, the Bank of England targets inflation. By granting independence, inflation bias can be eliminated.

Test yourself

Q1. What is the cause of inflation bias?

Q2. What effect might we expect inflation rate targeting by the central bank to have on inflation and unemployment?

Chapter summary – pulling it all together

By the end of this chapter you should be able to:

	Confident ✓	Not confident?
Explain labour market concepts such as the rate of unemployment, equilibrium unemployment and disequilibrium unemployment		Revise pages 142–147
Use a labour market diagram to illustrate equilibrium and disequilibrium unemployment		Revise pages 143–148
Explain what is meant by the rate of inflation and be able to identify different types of inflation		Revise pages 148–151
Describe the empirical Phillips curve relationship identified by A.W. Phillips		Revise pages 151–152

	Confident ✓	Not confident?
Explain the economic theory behind the possibility that the simple Phillips curve offers policy-makers a menu of choices over rates of inflation and unemployment		Revise pages 153–154
Explain how the expectations-augmented Phillips curve (EAPC) can result in the accelerationist hypothesis		Revise pages 155–159
Explain what is meant by rational expectations and how, in conjunction with assumptions about the determination of input prices, the inflation–unemployment trade-off is affected		Revise pages 159–161
Apply the EAPC framework to explain the concepts of inflation bias and the move in many countries towards some form of central bank independence		Revise pages 161–163

Now try the assessment question at the start of this chapter, using the answer guidelines below.

Answer guidelines

✱ Assessment question

Does the Phillips curve relationship demonstrate that policy-makers can trade off lower unemployment against higher inflation?

Approaching the question

The question invites you undertake a policy-focused discussion while embedding within your answer key macroeconomic concepts and ideas. It is important to recognise that while engaging in a discussion it is suitably anchored in economic theory.

Important points to include

- **The Phillips curve relationship.** Describe the empirical relationship that Phillips found between the rate of unemployment and wage inflation and how this seemed to provide policy-makers with macroeconomic choices.

- **Economics behind the Phillips curve.** Discuss the economics behind the Phillips curve that would allow policy-makers to trade off lower unemployment (below the equilibrium rate) against higher inflation.

- **Expectations-augmented Phillips curve (EAPC).** With reference to the expectations-augmented Phillips curve, explore the significance of inflation rate expectations and of wage-setting behaviour on our understanding of the inflation–unemployment trade-off. In doing so, illustrate the accelerationist hypothesis and the possibility of a vertical long-run Phillips curve.

- **Central bank independence.** Explain how economic thinking on the Phillips curve relationship has seen many countries grant their central bank some form of independence over monetary policy. Reference should be made to the concept of inflation bias.

Make your answer stand out

- Embed economic theory within your answer. Avoid simply 'presenting' the Phillips curve. Think about the economic theory behind it. This theory has generated keenly contested debates between economists over the ability of policy-makers to exploit an unemployment–inflation trade-off. Analyse the link between the *AD–AS* framework and the Phillips curve.

- Ensure that key concepts are properly explained. For instance, ensure that you carefully explain what is meant by terms such as the rate of inflation, the rate of unemployment, equilibrium unemployment, adaptive expectations, the accelerationist hypothesis, rational expectations and surprise inflation.

- Draw conclusions. The question is inviting a considered opinion!

Read to impress

Here are some books, articles and other sources that you can use to develop your answers on the topic area.

Books

Griffiths, A. and Wall, S. (2012) *Applied Economics*, 12th edition, Chapter 22, 'Inflation'. Harlow, UK: Pearson Education.

Griffiths, A. and Wall, S. (2012) *Applied Economics*, 12th edition, Chapter 23, 'Unemployment'. Harlow, UK: Pearson Education.

Parkin, M., Powell, M. and Matthews, K. (2012) *Essential Economics*, European edition, Chapter 11, 'Monitoring jobs and inflation'. Harlow, UK: Pearson Education.

Parkin, M., Powell, M. and Matthews, K. (2012) *Essential Economics*, European edition, Chapter 15, 'Growth, inflation and cycles'. Harlow, UK: Pearson Education.

Sloman, J. and Garratt, D. (2013) *Essentials of Economics*, 6th edition, Chapter 11, 'Inflation and unemployment'. Harlow, UK: Pearson Education.

Articles

Benito, A. and Bunn, P. (2011) Understanding labour force participation in the United Kingdom. *Bank of England Quarterly Bulletin*, Q1: 36–42 (www.bankofengland.co.uk/publications/Documents/quarterlybulletin/qb110102.pdf).

Faccini, R. and Hackworth, C. (2010) Changes in output, employment and wages during recessions in the United Kingdom. *Bank of England Quarterly Bulletin*, Q1: 43–50 (www.bankofengland.co.uk/publications/Documents/quarterlybulletin/qb100103.pdf).

Greenslade, J. and Parker, M. (2008) Price setting behaviour in the United Kingdom. *Bank of England Quarterly Bulletin*, Q4: 404–14 (www.bankofengland.co.uk/publications/Documents/quarterlybulletin/qb080403.pdf).

Periodicals and newspapers

The Bank of England's *Inflation Report* contains a readable overview of recent patterns in the national economy, including the Bank's considered opinions on the prospects for inflation.

An accessible commentary with figures relating to all aspects of the UK labour market is the *Statistical Bulletin: Labour Market Statistics* published monthly by the Office for National Statistics. This and other related information can be accessed at: www.ons.gov.uk/ons/taxonomy/index.html?nscl=Labour+Market.

An accessible commentary with figures relating to UK consumer prices is the *Statistical Bulletin: Consumer Price Indices* published monthly by the Office for National Statistics. This and other related information can be accessed at: www.ons.gov.uk/ons/taxonomy/index.html?nscl=Price+Indices+and+Inflation.

BBC News (2012) UK productivity puzzle baffles economists. Andrew Walker, 18 October.

Financial Times (2011) QE3 on its way as Fed prepares Phillips Trial. Scott Minerd, 1 November.

Financial Times (2012) Inflation puts pressure on Bank of England. Jamie Chisholm, 13 November.

Financial Times (2012) One in 10 workers now underemployed. Brian Groom, 28 November.

Financial Times (2012) Job preservation key in UK downturn. Brian Groom, 29 November.

Companion website

Go to the companion website at **www.pearson.co.uk/econexpress** to find more revision support online for this topic area.

Notes

Notes

7

The open economy

Topic map

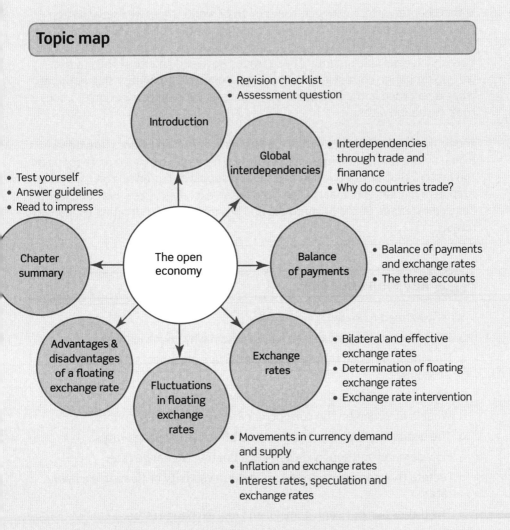

- Revision checklist
- Assessment question

Introduction

Global interdependencies
- Interdependencies through trade and finanance
- Why do countries trade?

- Test yourself
- Answer guidelines
- Read to impress

The open economy

Chapter summary

Balance of payments
- Balance of payments and exchange rates
- The three accounts

Advantages & disadvantages of a floating exchange rate

Fluctuations in floating exchange rates

Exchange rates
- Bilateral and effective exchange rates
- Determination of floating exchange rates
- Exchange rate intervention

- Movements in currency demand and supply
- Inflation and exchange rates
- Interest rates, speculation and exchange rates

A printable version of this topic map is available from **www.pearsoned.co.uk/econexpress**

Introduction

We live in an incredibly interdependent world. Economic interdependence occurs primarily through trade in goods and services or through finance. Economic events in one country can have important consequences for another. A comparison of many countries' business cycles will frequently show similar peaks and troughs. This can hardly be clearer than when comparing growth rates in the late 2000s and early 2010s. The financial crisis of the late 2000s spread like a contagion, making for a global economic downturn.

In this chapter, after looking at the growth of world trade, we focus first on the balance of payments. The balance of payments allows us to look at a record of a country's trade in goods and services and its cross-border transactions in financial instruments. These trades between countries require that we can exchange currencies. We therefore consider the relationship between what is recorded in the balance of payments and the determination of countries' exchange rates.

Today, most countries allow their currencies to 'float' and, hence, are determined by the forces of demand and supply. Therefore, we move on to focus on the factors that affect the demand for and supply of currencies on the foreign exchange market and analyse their impact on exchange rates. We conclude by considering some of the advantages and disadvantages of floating exchange rates.

Revision checklist

What you need to know:

- ❏ How comparative advantage helps explain why countries trade.
- ❏ How independence through trade and finance connects national economies.
- ❏ What is recorded on the balance of payments.
- ❏ What is recorded on the current, capital and financial accounts.
- ❏ The distinction between bilateral and effective exchange rates.
- ❏ How demand and supply determine a floating exchange rate.
- ❏ Factors that contribute to the short-term volatility of floating exchange rates.
- ❏ The distinction between nominal and real exchange rates.
- ❏ The advantages and disadvantages of floating exchange rates.

Assessment question

Can you answer this essay-type question? Guidelines on answering the question are presented at the end of this chapter.

What factors help to determine a currency's exchange rate? How can we explain the commonly observed volatility of exchange rates?

Global interdependencies

Interdependence through trade and finance

The economic fortunes of countries are linked in two principal ways. First, there is interdependence through trade. Second, there is interdependence through financial institutions and markets.

Consider first interdependence through trade. In 2011, the *value* of world merchandise exports was estimated at US$18.3 trillion. The average annual rate of increase in the value of merchandise exports between 1951 and 2011 was 10¼ per cent. If we strip out the effect of inflation, we find that the average annual rate of increase in the *volume* of merchandise exports over this period was 6 per cent.

Figure 7.1 shows the annual rate of growth in the volume of merchandise exports alongside global output (real GDP). While the volume of exports has grown by 6 per cent per year over the last 60 years, the average growth in world output has been just a little over 3½ per cent. Countries' trade flows have become increasingly large relative to their output. Therefore, economies have become increasingly 'open' to trade in goods and services.

Another important form of interconnectedness between countries occurs through financial institutions and markets. The global nature of these institutions and markets, along with the removal of barriers to financial instruments being traded between countries, has meant that cross-border financial flows have grown even more quickly than trade flows.

Many of these international financial flows are sensitive to movements in countries' interest rates and countries' exchange rates (see below). Global finance has been an important source of funds for banks looking to expand their lending opportunities. As we saw earlier (Chapter 5), banks have increasingly securitised parts of their portfolio of assets, such as residential mortgages. This means that they have been able to transform otherwise fairly

Figure 7.1 Annual growth in world merchandise exports and GDP by volume (%).
Source: Based on data in *International Trade Statistics 2012*, Appendix, Table A1a, World Trade Organization.

illiquid assets into tradable financial instruments, known as collateralised debt obligations (CDOs), to raise funds for further lending.

Today's global financial system is characterised by a complex chain of interdependencies between financial institutions and financial markets. This is most starkly demonstrated by the financial crisis of the late 2000s. Some of the income streams behind CDOs began to dry up as the original borrowers, largely US homeowners, began to default on their payments. The international scale of investment through CDOs meant that the problem spread like a contagion across the globe.

As countries' interconnectedness has increased, we frequently observe similar patterns in individual countries' output to those in global output. Therefore, the world economy experiences fluctuations in economic growth, as we can see in Figure 7.1. This **international business cycle** is frequently mirrored in the business cycle of individual countries.

Key definition

International business cycle
Fluctuations in global output that are frequently mirrored by national economies.

Why do countries trade?

An important reason behind why countries trade is the quantity and effectiveness of their own factors of production. For example, there are often significant differences between countries in labour skills, the types of capital equipment, access to raw materials and climate, etc. Some of these differences persist, such as access to raw materials and countries' climates. On the other hand, some differences, such as differences in labour skills, are potentially less permanent though they can nonetheless persist for some time. The result is that different countries are more or less effective than others in supplying goods and services.

The key point here is that the *relative* cost of producing goods varies from one country to another. Therefore, the goods sacrificed in producing one unit of a particular good vary across countries. In other words, the opportunity cost in the production of goods varies. The **law of comparative advantage** states that countries can gain by *specialising* in producing and then exporting those goods in which they have a relatively low opportunity cost as compared with other countries.

Key definition

Law of comparative advantage

The potential for two countries to gain from trade because of differences in their opportunity costs of producing various goods.

A significant countervailing effect on countries specialising is *increasing* opportunity costs in production. This occurs at a point when, in specialising in the production of a good, a country begins to use resources that are increasingly less effective or better suited to alternative uses. For instance, it is more effective for a manufacturing powerhouse like Germany to use its fertile agriculture land to produce food rather than to use this land to produce even more manufactured goods. Consequently, there is typically a limit to specialisation.

Recap

World trade has grown more rapidly than global output. Global interdependencies arise from interdependencies through trade and finance. Countries can gain from trading in those goods in which the opportunity cost of their production is lower than that of other countries.

Q1. What is meant by an international business cycle? What might affect the extent to which any one country's business cycle mirrors the international business cycle?

Q2. Can two countries gain from trading with each other if one of the countries needs fewer resources to produce tradable goods?

Balance of payments

Balance of payments and exchange rates

The balance of payments is a record of all the flows of money between a country's residents and the rest of the world. Inflows represent credits on the balance of payments and outflows represent debits.

Credit items on a country's balance of payments create a demand for that country's currency on the foreign exchange market. For instance, foreign residents looking to buy British goods or assets will need British pounds in order to complete the transaction.

Debit items on a country's balance of payments create a supply of that country's currency on the foreign exchange market. For instance, UK residents looking to purchase foreign goods or assets will need foreign currency in order to complete the transaction. They will therefore supply British pounds in exchange for foreign currency.

The three accounts

There are three main parts of the balance of payments account: the *current account*, the *capital account* and the *financial account*. Table 7.1 shows the UK balance of payments for 2011.

The **current account** relates to the flow of money incomes. It too comprises three parts:

● *Balance of trade (in goods and services)*. This records payments for exports (*X*) and imports (*M*). Exports are a credit item and imports are a debit item on the balance of payments. Where exports exceed imports, a country runs a balance of trade surplus (*X* > *M*). If its imports exceed its exports it runs a balance of trade deficit (*M* > *X*).

● *Net income flows*. These are flows of money between countries in the form of wages, profits and interest. For instance, dividend payments

Table 7.1 UK balance of payments, 2012.

	£m	% of GDP
CURRENT ACCOUNT		
Balance on trade in goods	−106,343	−6.9
Balance on trade in services	70,189	4.6
Balance of trade	**−36,154**	**−2.3**
Income balance	1,561	0.1
Net current transfers	−23,087	−1.5
Current account balance	**−57,679**	**−3.7**
CAPITAL ACCOUNT		
Capital account balance	**3,705**	**0.2**
FINANCIAL ACCOUNT		
Net direct investment	−5,738	−0.4
Portfolio investment balance	−203,375	−13.2
Other investment balance	234,493	15.2
Balance of financial derivatives	30,759	2.0
Reserve assets	−7,642	−0.5
Financial account balance	**48,497**	**3.1**
Net errors and omissions	**5,477**	**0.4**
Balance	0	0

Source: Based on data from *Balance of Payments quarterly First Release*, National Statistics and *Quarterly National Accounts*, National Statistics.

earned by UK residents on their holdings of shares in foreign companies are a credit item.

- *Current transfers of money* between countries. These are transfers for the purpose of consumption. For instance, a transfer payment by the British government to an overseas organisation is a debit item whereas a payment by a foreign family to a student studying in the UK is a credit item.

The **capital account** records the transfer of ownership of *non-produced, non-financial assets* as well as *capital transfers*. First, it records the flows of funds associated with the transfer of ownership of certain fixed assets, including the rights to natural resources and the land purchases and sales associated with foreign embassies. Second, it includes the transfer of intangibles such as patents, copyrights and trademarks. Third, it records money transfers intended for investment, including official debt forgiveness and the money brought into the economy by migrants. The capital account is small in comparison with the current and financial accounts.

Finally, the **financial account** records transactions in financial assets and liabilities. This comprises three principal types of financial flows:

- *Direct investment.* Capital investment constituting at least 10 per cent or more of ordinary shares or voting stock (otherwise it is portfolio investment). Capital invested in a domestic enterprise by a foreign investor is inward direct investment and capital invested by a domestic investor in an overseas enterprise is outward direct investment.

- *Portfolio investment.* Investment involving transactions in securities. This includes transactions in share capital, bills or bonds.

- *Other investment and financial flows.* Short-term financial flows. These consist primarily of deposits and loans involving monetary financial institutions (MFIs) and dealers in securities (tradable financial instruments). These flows are sensitive to changes in countries' interest rates and in exchange rates.

- *Financial derivatives.* These are financial instruments that are 'linked' to a financial instrument or to a commodity. They enable parties to enter into contracts to insure themselves against specific risks such as interest rate risk, currency movements or changes in commodity prices.

- *Flows to and from reserves.* The UK's reserves of gold and foreign currency assets are held in a Bank of England account known as the Exchange Equalisation Account. It can be used to reduce fluctuations in the exchange rate. Drawing on reserves appears as a *credit* item in the balance of payments accounts since it represents an *inflow* to the balance of payments. Conversely, additions to a country's reserves appear as a debit item.

Key definitions

Current account

The balance of trade in goods and services, plus net income flows and current transfers of money.

Capital account

A record of the transfer of ownership of non-produced, non-financial assets and of capital transfers.

Financial account

A record of cross-border transactions involving financial instruments, such as deposits with financial institutions.

Taken together the sum of the current, capital and financial accounts should be zero. The exchange rate adjusts to bring this about (or governments would need to intervene). As we shall see shortly, exchange rates move in response to changes in the demand for and supply of countries' currencies.

However, given the number of sources from which the data are collected, a *net errors and omission item* is used to ensure balance. Table 7.1 summarises the UK balance of payments for 2012. From it, we can see that the UK ran a substantial current account deficit. This was largely offset by a surplus on the financial account.

Figure 7.2 provides an historical perspective of the UK balance of payments. It shows that a current account deficit has persisted since the mid-1980s. This is consistent with a longer-term pattern rather than merely fluctuations accompanying the economy's business cycle. These fluctuations can occur because the demand for imports is positively related to national income (see Chapter 2). Therefore, stronger domestic economic growth can cause the current account to deteriorate as import consumption increases.

 Assessment advice

The balance of payments contains many, many numbers. Do not try to remember each one of them! Instead, focus first on understanding what is recorded in the balance of payment accounts. Then try to form a general sense of the composition of the balance of payments in the UK, noting, in particular, any longer-term patterns.

Recap

The balance of payments is a record of cross-border transactions. It can be broken down into three separate accounts: the current account, the capital account and the financial account. The UK has for some time run a current account deficit balanced by a financial account surplus.

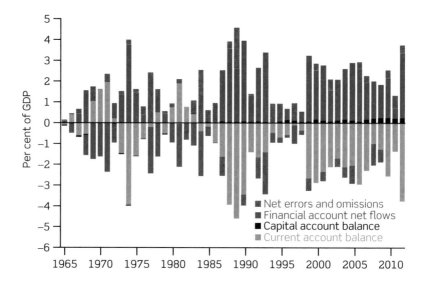

Figure 7.2 UK balance of payments as a percentage of GDP.

Source: Based on data from *Balance of Payments quarterly First Release* and *Quarterly National Accounts*, National Statistics.

Test yourself

Q1. Explain how the three sub-accounts of the balance of payments differ.

Q2. What relationship exists between the items recorded in the balance of payments and the transactions on the foreign exchange market?

Exchange rates

Bilateral and effective exchange rates

The balance of payments records the cross-border flows of money. These transactions involve numerous currencies. Foreign residents looking to visit the UK will need British pounds, as will a foreign company importing UK goods or a foreign investor buying British stocks and shares. Similarly, UK residents will need foreign currency with which to purchase foreign goods or assets.

UK residents purchasing foreign currency with British pounds need to go to a foreign exchange dealer. They will be quoted an exchange rate at which the domestic currency, British pounds (£), will be exchanged for foreign currency, say US dollars ($). An exchange rate of £1 = $1.75 means that £1 will purchase $1.75. This is an example of a **bilateral exchange rate**, the rate at which two currencies can be exchanged.

Exchange rates are constantly changing as foreign exchange dealers balance the amount of the various currencies they purchase (customers sell) to the amount they sell (customers demand). Consequently, exchange rates move in line with changes in demand and supply.

✳ Assessment advice

Confusion can result from alternative presentations of exchange rates. Take some time to understand the format used in this chapter: that is, *the foreign currency price of the domestic currency*. For example, the foreign currency price of the British pound could be the number of euros per £1, Swiss francs per £1 or US dollars per £1.

Although we can view the price of one currency against another, it is often advantageous to look at a weighted average exchange rate against a bundle of currencies where the weights reflect the amount of trade with other countries. A trade-weighted exchange rate index is known as an **effective exchange rate**.

Figure 7.3 shows the effective exchange rate index for the UK since 1970. It captures nicely the marked fluctuations typically observed in exchange rates.

Figure 7.3 UK effective exchange rate index, 2010 = 100.

Source: Bank for International Settlements.

Key definitions

Bilateral exchange rate

The rate at which two currencies can be exchanged.

Effective exchange rate

A trade-weighted average exchange rate allowing us to compare a country's currency with a bundle of other currencies.

Determination of floating exchange rates

So what causes exchange rates to fluctuate? In a 'free market', that is without government intervention in the foreign exchange market, exchange rates are determined by demand and supply. An exchange rate determined by the forces of demand and supply is a **floating exchange rate**.

Key definition

Floating exchange rate

Where exchange rates are determined by demand and supply without government intervention in the foreign exchange market.

To understand the factors influencing the rate at which currencies exchange we begin by assuming that there are just two countries: the UK and USA. We will consider what affects the number of US dollars that can be exchanged for £1, i.e. the US dollar price of the British pound.

The *demand* for British pounds arises when American residents wish to purchase British goods or assets. They will need to exchange their US dollars for British pounds. The higher the US dollar price of British pounds, the more US dollars that are needed to purchase a given amount of British pounds. Consequently, the higher the exchange rate (the higher the US dollar price of the British pound), the more expensive it is for American residents to obtain British goods and assets. The demand curve (D_1) for British pounds is therefore drawn as downward sloping.

The *supply* of British pounds arises when UK residents wish to obtain American goods and services. The higher the exchange rate, the more US dollars the UK residents get for their British pounds. This makes American goods and assets relatively cheaper to obtain. Consequently, the higher the exchange rate (the higher the US dollar price of the British pound), the more British pounds, others things being equal, that are supplied. The supply curve (S_1) for British pounds is therefore drawn as upward sloping.

In Figure 7.4 the equilibrium exchange rate is E_1 where $1.75 can be exchanged for £1. At a higher exchange rate, say $2 to £1, the supply of British pounds exceeds the demand for British pounds. This is because the high US dollar price of British pounds is deterring American residents from obtaining British goods and assets, while encouraging British residents to purchase American goods and assets. Consequently, there is an excess supply of British pounds. Foreign exchange dealers therefore have an incentive to lower the exchange rate, thereby encouraging a greater demand for British pounds and reducing their excess holding of British pounds.

At a lower exchange rate, say $1.5 to £1, there would be an excess demand for pounds. Foreign exchange dealers would find themselves with a shortage of pounds. This is because the lower American dollar price of the pound would deter British residents from purchasing the now more expensive American goods and assets. On the other hand, American residents would be attracted by the relatively lower price of British goods and assets.

Recap

A bilateral exchange rate refers to the rate of exchange between two currencies. An effective exchange rate is an index allowing us to track the trade-weighted average foreign currency price of a particular currency, such as the British pound. The demand for a domestic currency on the foreign exchange market arises when foreign residents purchase domestic goods and assets. Domestic residents purchasing foreign goods and assets create the supply of the domestic currency. The equilibrium exchange rate balances demand and supply.

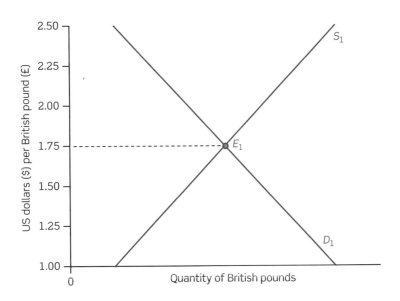

Figure 7.4 Determination of floating exchange rate.

Q1. Explain the derivation of the demand and supply curves for currencies on the foreign exchange market.

Q2. What is in 'balance' at the equilibrium exchange rate? Explain the mechanism by which the actual exchange rate would move towards equilibrium if it were currently below the equilibrium rate.

Exchange rate intervention

As Figure 7.3 shows, exchange rates can be volatile in the short term. Governments or central banks may wish to intervene to reduce this volatility. Occasional interventions by the authorities result in a **managed float**, sometimes referred to as a *dirty float*.

Alternatively, the authorities may intervene as necessary to target a specific exchange rate. They may wish to fix their exchange rate below the current equilibrium in order to make the country's exports relatively more attractive to foreign residents. However, they may want to fix the rate above the current equilibrium to counter the effects of import prices on domestic inflation. This form of intervention is known as a **fixed exchange rate regime**.

Managed float (dirty float)

A system of floating exchange rates where the authorities occasionally intervene to affect exchange rates.

Fixed exchange rate regime

Where the authorities intervene in an attempt to 'fix' the exchange rate at a specific level.

Consider now Figure 7.5. Assume that the authorities want to maintain a fixed exchange rate at $1.5 to £1. This is *below* the current equilibrium rate of $1.75 to £1. One way they could look to achieve this is by selling *additional* British pounds on the foreign exchange market in exchange for US dollars equivalent to the horizontal distance $(b - a)$. In doing so, the authorities would be building up their reserves of foreign currency and also increasing the money supply.

If the authorities had wanted to maintain an exchange rate *above* the current equilibrium at say $2 to £1, they would need to purchase excess pounds equivalent to the horizontal distance $(d - c)$. They could do this by drawing on their foreign currency reserves. All other things being equal, this would have the effect of decreasing the money supply.

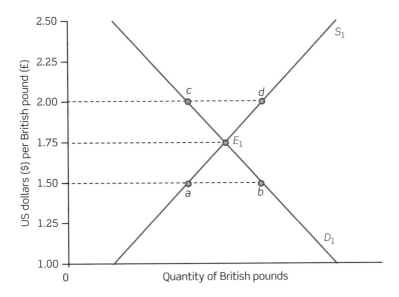

Figure 7.5 Fixed exchange rate.

Given that the funds available to international investors are huge and highly mobile, the selling or purchasing of foreign exchange reserves by the central bank to manage the exchange rate is only ever likely to be sustainable in the short term. There is a limit to the stock of currency reserves. Instead, in the longer term the central bank may turn to interest rates to try and manage the exchange rate.

Assume that the Bank of England wants to maintain an exchange rate of $1.50 to £1 and so below the equilibrium rate. An alternative strategy would be for the Bank of England to cut interest rates. This will deter foreign investors from depositing money in the UK and encourage UK investors to deposit money abroad. This induces two effects. First, the demand for British pounds on the foreign exchange markets falls, causing the demand curve, D_1 in Figure 7.5, to move leftwards. Second, the supply of British pounds by UK residents increases, causing the supply curve, S_1, to move rightwards.

Managing the exchange rate can conflict with other economic objectives. For instance, the effect of the lower interest rates needed to keep the exchange rate below equilibrium could be higher domestic inflation rates. Lower interest rates tend to increase spending by domestic residents, thereby resulting in higher domestic prices. However, the central bank is unable to raise interest rates to reduce domestic inflation because to do so would mean that that the exchange rate would rise.

The principal reason why the central bank could not raise interest rates in this situation is the response of investors, largely financial institutions. Domestic investors would respond to the relatively higher interest rate by switching their investments from abroad (decreasing the supply of British pounds in Figure 7.5) while foreign investors would move investments into the UK (increasing the demand for British pounds). This effect is likely to be significant in an age of rapid and large financial flows across national borders. Hence, highly mobile financial capital can create a policy dilemma for authorities looking to manage exchange rates.

Recap

The authorities may intervene in the foreign exchange market to manage the exchange rate, to limit its volatility, or alternatively to fix the exchange rate at a specific value. This may involve the use by the authorities of foreign exchange reserves or the purposeful setting of domestic interest rates to target the exchange rate.

Test yourself

Q1. Using a demand–supply diagram, explain how the authorities could use foreign exchange reserves to keep the exchange rate above its equilibrium level.

Q2. What problems do the authorities face in fixing an exchange rate for a prolonged period?

Fluctuations in exchange rates

Movements in currency demand and supply

Where exchange rates are allowed to move freely they are determined by demand and supply. As we saw above, the demand for foreign currency relates to the credit items on the balance of payments and the supply of domestic currency relates to the debit items on the balance of payments. Under a floating exchange rate, changes in the exchange rate enable the balance of payments to balance. A rise in the free-market exchange rate is known as an **appreciation**, and a fall in the free-market exchange rate is known as a **depreciation**.

Key definitions

Appreciation
A rise in the free-market exchange rate of the domestic currency against foreign currencies.

Depreciation

A fall in the free-market exchange rate of the domestic currency against foreign currencies.

To understand better the movements in exchange rates we return to our two-country case: the UK and USA. The following are possible causes of an *appreciation* of the British pound against the US dollar:

- *Lower domestic inflation rates.* If the average price of British goods rises less quickly than that of American goods, UK exports become more attractive relative to their US counterparts. This increases the demand for British pounds. This will result in a rightward movement of the demand curve in Figure 7.6, such as that from D_1 to D_2. With a lower demand by UK residents for American goods, the supply of British pounds will decrease. This will result in a leftward movement of the supply curve in Figure 7.6, such as that from S_1 to S_2.

- *Higher domestic interest rates.* If UK interest rates were to rise *relative* to US interest rates, UK deposits become more attractive relative to their US counterparts. Consequently, more American residents, other things remaining equal, will deposit their money in the UK. This increases the demand for British pounds (D_1 to D_2). On the other hand, the demand by UK residents for American investments decreases. This decreases the supply of British pounds (S_1 to S_2).

- *Weaker domestic economic growth.* If economic growth is stronger in the USA than in the UK, American demand for UK exports will grow relative to British demand for US exports. Again, the effect is to increase the demand by Americans for British pounds (D_1 to D_2) and reduce the supply of pounds by UK residents (S_1 to S_2).

- *Speculation of an appreciation.* If there is speculation that the exchange rate will rise, there will be an increase in the current demand for British pounds by US investors (D_1 to D_2). If the exchange rate does then appreciate they will be able to convert their holdings of British pounds into a larger amount of US dollars. Similarly, there will be a fall in the supply of British pounds by UK businesses and financial institutions (S_1 to S_2).

Recap

Changes in a floating exchange rate are caused by changes in demand and supply on foreign currency markets. Factors behind these changes include *relative* rates of inflation, nominal interest rates and economic growth. Speculation concerning future exchange rates can result in significant movements in current exchange rates.

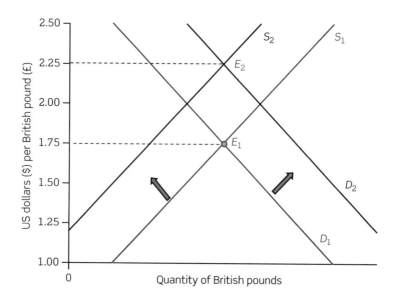

Figure 7.6 An example of an appreciating exchange rate.

Nominal and real effective exchange rates

So far, our focus has been on the *nominal* exchange rate: the actual rate at which one currency exchanges for another. It is the rate we observe. If we want to get a sense of the volume of imports a country can obtain from selling a given volume of exports, we need also to take into account what is happening to the average (domestic currency) price of exports relative to the trade-weighted average (foreign currency) price of imports.

The **real exchange rate** is adjusted for the average prices of exports and imports. For example, if the average price of a country's exports rises relative to the average price of its imports, the real effective exchange rate (E_R) will rise relative to its nominal effective exchange rate (E_N). The country is now able to obtain a larger volume of imports from selling a given volume of exports.

We can write the real effective exchange rate as

$$E_R = E_N \times (P_X / P_M) \tag{7.1}$$

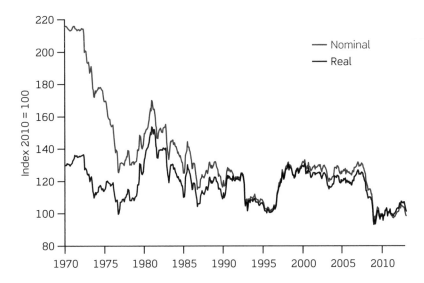

Figure 7.7 UK nominal and real effective exchange rate index, 2010 = 100.

Source: Bank for International Settlements.

where P_X is the average (domestic currency) price of exports and P_M is the trade-weighted average (foreign currency) price of imports.

We can also use the real exchange rate to analyse the competitiveness of a country's exports. The higher the real exchange rate, the less competitive a country's exports. Figure 7.7 shows the real effective exchange rate index for the British pound alongside the nominal effective exchange rate index since 1970. Marked short-term fluctuations are observed in both the nominal *and* real effective exchange rates.

Key definition

Real exchange rate

The actual exchange rate adjusted by the average price of a country's exports relative to the average price of its imports.

Examples & evidence

The depreciation of the British pound from 2007

The late 2000s saw a significant depreciation of the effective exchange rate for the British pound. The chart over the page plots the *nominal* and *real* effective exchange rates for the British pound from 2006. It captures nicely how, from around the autumn of 2007, the effective exchange rate began to fall sharply.

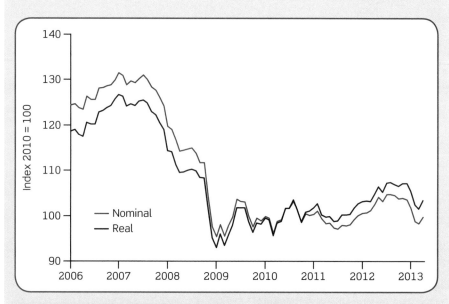

Nominal and real effective exchange rates from 2006.
Source: Bank for International Settlements.

Over the period from September 2007 to January 2009, the nominal effective exchange rate fell by 26 per cent while the real exchange rate, after adjusting for the relative price of exports to imports, fell by 24 per cent. Therefore, over a period during which the British financial system was rocked by the financial crisis, the British pound lost about one-quarter of its value.

There was to be no immediate return of the effective exchange rate to pre-financial-crisis values. This was despite a mild appreciation of the British pound between July 2011 and September 2012. Over this period the nominal effective exchange rate appreciated by 6.8 per cent while the real rate appreciated by 7.8 per cent. Nonetheless, if we compare September 2012 with September 2007, the nominal effective exchange rate for the British pound was 19 per cent lower while the real effective exchange rate was 13 per cent lower. If we compare this with the trade-weighted exchange rate indices of other countries in the table below, this amounted to a major competitive boost for UK exporters.

Percentage change in effective exchange rate, September 2007 to September 2012

	Nominal	Real
UK	−18.6	−13.1
Australia	17.1	23.6
Canada	4.2	3.0

	Nominal	Real
Germany	−4.8	−6.4
Ireland	−2.9	−11.0
Singapore	17.1	30.6
Switzerland	31.9	21.5
USA	−4.2	−1.3

Source: Based on data from Bank for International Settlements.

Questions

1. What factors might have contributed to the significant *depreciation* of the British pound in the late 2000s?
2. What factors might help explain the significant *appreciation* of the Swiss franc in the late 2000s?

Inflation and exchange rates

We identified earlier that differences in countries' inflation rates can generate movements in nominal exchange rates. Changes in nominal exchange rates can help countries with higher inflation rates remain internationally competitive. To see why, consider the extreme case where a country's GDP deflator (the economy's average price level) doubles but where the foreign inflation rate is zero. Assume that the nominal (actual) exchange rate remains unchanged so that we observe the average price of the country's exportable goods (P_X) double relative to the average foreign currency price of its imports (P_M). Consequently, foreign residents will need to exchange double the amount of foreign currency units into British pounds to purchase the same volume of British goods as before.

With British exports now relatively more expensive, foreign demand will tend to fall. This reduces the demand for British pounds. However, with foreign goods and assets now more attractive to UK residents, the supply of British pounds on the foreign exchange markets will rise. The fall in demand and increase in supply of British pounds will cause the nominal exchange rate to fall. As the foreign currency price of British pounds falls, the competitiveness of British exports starts to rise. If the nominal exchange rate (E_N) was to halve, then with the average price of exports to imports, P_X/P_M, having doubled, the real exchange rate would be unchanged (see equation 7.1).

The theory of **purchasing-power parity** (PPP) suggests that changes in domestic price levels relative to foreign price levels will be offset by changes in the *nominal* exchange rate. Countries with higher-than-average inflation

189

rates will, other things being equal, experience a nominal depreciation in their currency against the currencies of those countries with lower-than-average inflation rates.

Key definition

Purchasing-power parity

The idea that the nominal exchange rate adjusts to offset differences in countries' inflation rates.

If we look at Figure 7.8 we observe considerable volatility in countries' real effective exchange rates. This means that in the short run nominal exchange rates move more than prices. Hence, short-run nominal exchange rate movements are the result of more than just countries' relative inflation rates.

Although they may be volatile in the short run, there is some evidence that in the longer term countries' real exchange rates move towards an equilibrium rate. The **long-run real exchange rate** is the rate at which the economy achieves both **internal balance** and **external balance**. Internal balance occurs when an economy's aggregate demand equals its potential output. External balance occurs when an economy's current account is in balance. Under a floating exchange rate the balance of payments is always zero. Therefore, an external balance also means that the sum of the capital and financial accounts is zero.

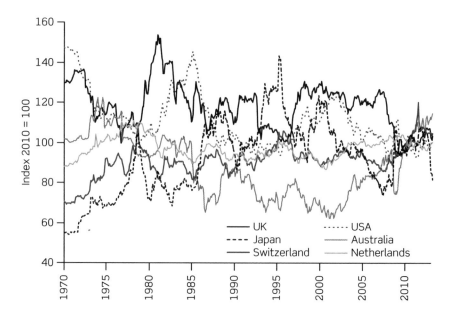

Figure 7.8 Real effective exchange rate indices, 2010 = 100.
Source: Bank for International Settlements.

Key definitions

Long-run equilibrium real exchange rate

The real exchange rate at which an economy achieves both internal and external balance.

Internal balance

The name given to the situation when an economy's aggregate demand equals its potential output.

External balance

The name given to the situation when the current account of the balance of payments is in balance.

✳ Assessment advice

An awareness of patterns and trends in relevant economic data can help to support your understanding of economic concepts and theories. In this context, try to keep up to date with the latest developments in exchange rates.

In the long run, with economies achieving both internal and external balance, the consumption by domestic residents ($C + I + G$) equals potential output. Therefore, the long-run income of an economy is determined by its potential output. Consequently, there will be a unique long-run real exchange rate when countries' current accounts are in balance. The real exchange rate determines the competitiveness of countries' exports. If the real rate was above the equilibrium rate, the current account would be in deficit. If the real rate was below the equilibrium rate, the current account would be in surplus.

However, the long-run equilibrium real exchange rate can itself change. This could be the result of longer-term changes in the structures of economies or technological progress. For instance, the discovery of new natural resources, such as oil and gas reserves, can result in an appreciation of the long-term real exchange rate. The increase in net exports following the discovery of the new resources requires a rise in the long-term real exchange rate to keep the overall current account in balance. Of course, this can disadvantage existing export markets. This is sometimes known as **Dutch disease** because, after the Dutch began mining natural gas reserves in the North Sea during the 1970s, the Dutch currency appreciated sharply (see Figure 7.8). A similar thing happened to the British pound when the UK began extracting gas and oil reserves from the North Sea.

> **Key definition**
>
> **Dutch disease**
> The name given to the appreciation of a currency following the discovery of new natural resources, which adversely impacts on existing export markets.

Interest rates, speculation and exchange rates

An important source of the short-term fluctuations in both nominal and real exchange rates is movements in finance. Over time, restrictions to cross-border financial flows have been removed. One consequence of this is that investors can readily switch funds between countries seeking out opportunities for profits. Differences between countries in the rates of interest on financial instruments have the potential to generate huge inflows or outflows. These flows can then generate significant fluctuations in exchange rates.

Differences between countries in their nominal interest rates do not in them-selves necessitate significant financial flows. Indeed, these differences may be necessary to prevent large financial flows! To understand this we need to consider the theory of **interest rate parity**. This states that differences in interest rates between countries on financial instruments should reflect expected movements in the currency in which the instrument is denominated.

> **Key definition**
>
> **Interest rate parity**
> The theory that international differences in interest rates should reflect expected movements in currencies.

Consider the case of an investor who has deposited British pounds with a financial institution in the UK and where the British pound is expected to depreciate. Investors will require a higher nominal interest rate in order to compensate them for the expected decline in the British pound. This is because they could have made a larger return by investing their money abroad in foreign assets offering the same nominal rate of return, waited for the Brit-ish pound to depreciate before then liquidating their asset and converting it back into British pounds. Therefore, if the British pound is expected to depreci-ate by 5 per cent against the US dollar over the coming year, an investor would need the return on an investment in the UK to be 5 percentage points higher compared with a similar investment in the USA.

Conversely, were the domestic currency expected to appreciate, then the nominal rate of interest on domestic assets would be lower than their international substitutes. If investors speculate that current interest rate differentials do not reflect expected movements in the exchange rate then huge financial flows will occur. Investors will simply switch funds between countries. These flows then generate significant volatility in the currency.

If investors believe that domestic interest rates are currently higher than necessary to equalise expected returns across countries, then investors will switch to domestic assets. This will cause the demand for the domestic currency on the foreign exchange market to rise and its supply to fall. Consequently, the currency will appreciate. However, when in due course investors look to realise their gains, the exchange rate will begin to fall.

✳ Assessment advice

The theories of *interest rate parity* and *purchasing-power parity* can be used to bring greater depth of analysis to an assessment on exchange rate determination.

Another form of speculative investment that can cause volatility in the real exchange rate or make it diverge from its longer-term equilibrium is known as the **carry trade**. This occurs when investors borrow funds from institutions in countries where interest rates are relatively low and invest them in assets in countries where interest rates are relatively high. For the carry trade to be profitable the interest rate differential needs to be greater than any expected depreciation of the currency in which the investors are investing. If a large number of investors undertake this type of activity, it can actually cause the domestic currency to appreciate further, making the carry trade very speculative and potentially very profitable. As with all speculative activity, timing is everything!

Key definition

Carry trade

Investors borrowing funds from countries with lower interest rates and investing them in countries with higher interest rates.

Figure 7.2 showed that the UK has experienced a persistent current account deficit since the mid-1980s. This has been offset by a financial account surplus. The UK has typically experienced relatively higher interest rates in comparison with countries like Germany and Japan, which have frequently run current account surpluses. Despite this current account deficit, the effective exchange rate for the British pound appreciated between January 1996 and January 2007 by 29 per cent in nominal terms and by 26 per cent in real terms (after adjusting for the prices of imports and exports).

In the short run, given the potential for huge international movements of finance, the transactions recorded on the financial account of the balance of payments are a crucial driver of the exchange rate. They can cause the real exchange rate to deviate significantly from its long-run equilibrium.

Recap

The real effective exchange is the nominal (actual) rate adjusted by the relative domestic currency price of exports compared with the foreign currency price of imports. We observe that both nominal and real exchange rates are volatile in the short run. In the short run, international financial flows can have huge significance for exchange rates. In the longer term, the real exchange rate may converge on an equilibrium rate. The equilibrium real exchange rate is the rate that ensures internal balance (aggregate demand equals potential output) and external balance (current account balance).

Test yourself

Q1. What does the theory of purchasing-power parity assume about movements in the nominal exchange rate?

Q2. Why is the removal of cross-border barriers to international finance potentially important for the behaviour of exchange rates?

Advantages and disadvantages of a floating exchange rate

As we saw above, both nominal and real floating exchange rates can be highly volatile in the short run. Therefore, one obvious disadvantage of floating as opposed to fixed exchange rates is their *instability*.

Exchange rate instability can be heightened by *speculation*. This can cause the real exchange rate to overshoot significantly its long-run equilibrium rate. Furthermore, changes to the exchange rate arising from shifts in demand and supply depend on how elastic (responsive) the demand and supply are to changes in the foreign currency price of the domestic currency.

To illustrate this, consider Figure 7.9. Assume that the existing exchange rate is $1.75 to £1 and that there is then an increase in the demand for British pounds. If the supply curve for British pounds is represented by S_2 rather than S_1 the appreciation of the currency is less. This is because the supply of the domestic currency on the foreign exchange market is more responsive to a change in the exchange rate. Hence, a smaller increase in the exchange rate is required for additional British pounds to come on to the foreign exchange market and meet the additional demand.

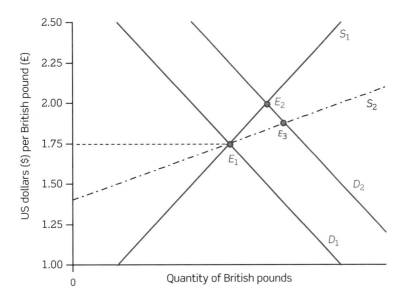

Figure 7.9 Elasticities and exchange rate volatility.

Exchange rate instability can cause *uncertainty* for businesses and investors. There is uncertainty about the expected returns on investments, including the worth of future profit streams. The possibility of a depreciation can be a deterrent to foreign investment.

Exchange rate instability can be partially overcome by entering into forward exchange contracts with financial institutions. In doing so, the two parties are agreeing to a rate of exchange at some point in the future. **Forward exchange rates** are typically negotiated for periods of up to one year.

Key definition

Forward exchange rates

Exchange rates agreed today at which currencies will be exchanged at some future point of time.

Fixed exchange rates can help to impose a discipline on domestic policy. Assume that the government relaxes fiscal policy and, because of rising domestic incomes, expenditure on imports rises, causing the current account to deteriorate. The deterioration of the current account puts downward pressure on the exchange rate as the supply of the domestic currency on the foreign exchange market rises.

Under a fixed exchange rate, the higher rate of inflation cannot be readily controlled by raising interest rates. This is because, in a world characterised by highly mobile financial capital, raising interest rates would attract huge inflows of financial capital, causing the domestic currency to appreciate sharply. Instead, in the short term, the government will need to deflate the economy by tightening fiscal policy to help maintain the exchange rate and reduce domestic inflation.

Although fixed exchange rates can help to promote fiscal discipline, the limited ability of the authorities to respond to changes in aggregate demand through monetary policy can cause prolonged deviations of the economy's output from its potential output. In other words, the impact of economic shocks could be prolonged under fixed exchange rates.

Assume this time that there has been a negative 'shock' to aggregate demand which causes the economy's output to fall and unemployment to rise. If fiscal policy were unchanged, the adjustment to restore internal balance would need to come from a downward move in wages and prices. As the relative price of the country's exports relative to the foreign currency price of its imports (P_X/P_M) fell, the competitiveness of the country's exports would improve. Therefore, with the nominal exchange rate fixed, lower prices would be needed to reduce the real exchange rate.

Although economies can adjust under a fixed exchange rate to economic shocks, a key question for policy-makers is how long such an adjustment process would take. A similar line of argument can be used when thinking about countries within a monetary union, such as those countries that make up the eurozone. The more inflexible the wages and prices of member countries in response to economic shocks, the more amplified or exaggerated their business cycles could be.

Recap

Floating exchange rates are volatile. This creates uncertainty for businesses and investors. Fixed exchange rates remove this volatility and can impose a discipline on the conduct of macroeconomic policy. However, where wages and prices are relatively inflexible, fixed exchange rates can mean that an economy's output deviates from its potential level for some considerable time.

Test yourself

Q1. Explain how a fixed exchange rate imposes discipline on the conduct of macroeconomic policy.

Q2. Under a fixed exchange rate regime, can the central bank adopt an inflation rate target?

Chapter summary – pulling it all together

By the end of this chapter you should be able to:

	Confident ✓	Not confident?
Explain the two principal types of economic interdependence between countries		Revise pages 171–172
Explain what is meant by comparative advantage and how it helps explain why countries trade		Revise pages 173–174
Describe what the current account, the capital account and the financial account of the balance of payments show		Revise pages 174–178
Explain the connection between the balance of payments and the demand for and supply of currencies on the foreign exchange markets		Revise pages 174 and 178–79
Define what is meant by a bilateral and an effective exchange rate		Revise pages 178–180
Draw a demand and supply diagram relating to the foreign exchange market		Revise pages 180–182
Explain how demand and supply help to determine a country's exchange rate		Revise pages 180–182
Identify factors that contribute to an appreciation or depreciation of a floating exchange rate		Revise pages 184–186
Explain the distinction between a nominal and a real exchange rate		Revise pages 186–189
Explore some of the reasons why floating exchange rates exhibit considerable volatility		Revise pages 189–194
Examine some of the advantages and disadvantages of floating exchange rates		Revise pages 182–184 and 194–196

Now try the assessment question at the start of this chapter, using the answer guidelines below.

Answer guidelines

✳ Assessment question

What factors help to determine a currency's exchange rate? How can we explain the commonly observed volatility of exchange rates?

Approaching the question

Despite being a question relating to an important macroeconomic topic, the question gives you an opportunity to apply the concepts of demand and supply.

Important points to include

- **Bilateral and effective exchange rates**. Explain clearly how foreign exchange rates are presented and how a trade-weighted average allows us to compare a single currency against a whole bundle of currencies.

- **The demand–supply framework.** With the aid of a diagram or diagrams, explain the derivation of the demand and supply curves in the foreign exchange market. Focus on why the demand curve for currency typically slopes downwards and the supply curve typically slopes upwards.

- **Applying demand and supply to illustrate fluctuations in the nominal exchange rate.** Using the demand–supply framework, identify some of the key variables that affect the nominal exchange rate. Show how the authorities could 'manage' the exchange rate.

- **Nominal and real exchange rates.** Distinguish between real and nominal exchange rates. Explain what is meant by the long-run equilibrium real exchange rate.

- **Explore theories of the determination of the exchange rate.** Analyse the alternative explanations of exchange rate determination including theories such as purchasing-power parity and interest rate parity.

Make your answer stand out

- Draw on real-world evidence in your discussion. For instance, show an awareness of patterns in the balance of payments of the UK (or other countries), in currency movements and in attempts by the authorities to manage exchange rates.

- Bring depth of analysis to your answer. For instance, in drawing on alternative explanations and empirical evidence you can attempt to demonstrate a broader mastery of the macroeconomy and of relevant macroeconomic concepts and theories.
- Draw conclusions. Based on the evidence and alternative explanations, can you draw any firm conclusions?

Read to impress

Here are some books, articles and other sources that you can use to develop your answers on the topic area.

Books

Griffiths, A. and Wall, S. (2012) *Applied Economics*, 12th edition, Chapter 25, 'Exchange rates and trade performance'. Harlow, UK: Pearson Education.

Sloman, J. and Garratt, D. (2013) *Essentials of Economics*, 6th edition, Chapter 13, 'Globalisation and international trade'. Harlow, UK: Pearson Education.

Sloman, J. and Garratt, D. (2013) *Essentials of Economics*, 6th edition, Chapter 14, 'Balance of payments and exchange rates'. Harlow, UK: Pearson Education.

Articles

Astley, M., Smith, J. and Pain, D. (2009) Interpreting recent movements in sterling. *Bank of England Quarterly Bulletin*, Q3: 202–14 (www.bankofengland.co.uk/publications/Documents/quarterlybulletin/qb090303.pdf).

Broderick, T. and Cox, C. (2010) The foreign exchange and over-the-counter interest rate derivatives markets in the United Kingdom. *Bank of England Quarterly Bulletin*, Q4: 354–65 (www.bankofengland.co.uk/publications/Documents/quarterlybulletin/qb100410.pdf).

Kamath, K. and Paul, V. (2011) Understanding recent developments in UK external trade. *Bank of England Quarterly Bulletin*, Q4: 294–304 (www.bankofengland.co.uk/publications/Documents/quarterlybulletin/qb110401.pdf).

O'Connor, J., Wackett, J. and Zammit, R. (2011) The use of foreign exchange markets by non-banks. *Bank of England Quarterly Bulletin*, Q2: 119–26. (www.bankofengland.co.uk/publications/Documents/quarterlybulletin/qb110204.pdf).

Periodicals and newspapers

The Bank of England's *Inflation Report* contains a readable overview of recent patterns in the both the domestic and global economies.

An accessible commentary with figures relating to all aspects of the UK balance of payments is the *Statistical Bulletin: Balance of Payments* published four times a year by the Office for National Statistics. This and other related information (including podcasts) can be accessed at: www.ons.gov.uk/ons/taxonomy/index.html?nscl=Balance+of+Payments.

Financial Times (2011) Britain needs to buy more from Bognor, not Barcelona. Chris Giles, 2 November.

Financial Times (2012) Britain in need of an export booster. Brian Groom, 23 October.

Financial Times (2012) Traders retreat as Brasilia steers real. Samantha Pearson, 29 November.

Financial Times (2012) Yen/won – currency clashes. 9 December.

Financial Times (2012) BOE Governor warns of currency wars. Chris Giles, 10 December.

Reuters (2013) Sterling eases versus dollar, focus turns to BOE. Phillip Baillie, 7 January.

Companion website

Go to the companion website at **www.pearsoned.co.uk/econexpress** to find more revision support online for this topic area.

Notes

Notes

And finally, before the assessment . . .

You should by now have developed your skills and knowledge in ways that can help you perform to the best of your ability, whatever the form of assessment used on your course.

At this stage you should be aware that your assessment involves one or more of the following.

- **Assignment** where one or more essay-type question(s) must be answered in your own time and to a specific word limit (e.g. 1,500 words)
- **Examination** where a timed test is set in a specified location with a range of possible questions, such as:
  - *Essay-type questions*
  - *Data response questions*
  - *Multiple choice questions*

Whatever the form of your assessment, the examiners will be looking to award marks for particular skills that you have displayed in your answers.

- **Application** The ability to apply knowledge of economic principles, theories or concepts to data or issues raised in the question. For example, you may be able to use demand, supply and elasticity concepts to explain why the price of gold is so volatile.
- **Analysis** The ability to identify the assumptions on which a particular line of reasoning depends. For example, you may be able to demonstrate that the benefits of a flexible exchange rate in achieving balance of payments equilibrium depend on there being sufficient price elasticity of demand for a country's exports and imports.
- **Evaluation** The ability to make reasoned judgements about the validity of different arguments. For example, you may be able to explain why some argue that austerity measures involving sharp reductions in budget deficits are needed for sustainable economic growth, whilst others argue that austerity measures must be abandoned if sustainable economic growth is to be achieved.

- **Synthesis** The ability to link ideas together in order to form a coherent and logical argument that is not immediately obvious. For example, you may be able to explain why the characteristics of the market in which the firm operates and the objectives the firm is pursuing must be identified if you are to understand the pricing behaviour of a particular firm.

How to approach and present assignments

Assignments will challenge you to write for different types of task, but the following steps will help you plan, structure and deliver your assignment whatever the task.

- **Realistic time planning:** Check the assignment submission date, work out how long you have from now to that date and allocate a specific amount of time each week to work on your assignment
- **Identify what you need to do:** Make sure you are clear on the word length, on the type of task (e.g. essay/report), on the topic (e.g. firm objective/economic growth) and on the instructions in the questions (e.g. assess/evaluate)

Here are some widely encountered instructions or 'command words' for assignments.

Instruction word	What you are expected to do
Analyse	Give an organised answer reviewing all aspects
Assess	Decide on relative value/importance of issues
Discuss	Give own thoughts and support your opinions or conclusions
Evaluate	Decide on merit of situation/argument and give a balanced judgement
Explain	Give reasons for
Review	Present facts and arguments

- **Find and use relevant materials:** Read and make notes on any readings/ sources provided on the assignment brief. The 'Read to impress' section at the end of each topic-based chapter in this book will help here.
- **Structure your assignment:** Make sure the following elements are present:
  - **Introduction:** *brief explanation of how you intend to approach the question, key definitions etc.*

- **Main body of the answer**: a clearly organised set of themes/issues relevant to the question (often using sub-headings)
- **Conclusions**: referring back to the original question, provide a review of the key points raised, perhaps with a balanced judgement
- **Reference accurately**: accurate and full referencing is a key part of any assignment and will help avoid any issue of plagiarism (i.e. taking credit for the work of others)
  - Identify and use a consistent referencing approach, e.g. Harvard style
  - Reference from the text wherever appropriate (e.g. Sloman, J. 2013) and provide full details of the source in your bibliography
  - Identify where you use exact words or sentences from a source using quotation marks or italics, followed by the source reference
- **Re-draft your material**: Try to give yourself time in your plan for redrafting your first attempt. The second or third draft will invariably be better than the first!

How to approach your examination

- Plan your revision: use a calendar to put dates on to your planner and write in the dates of your exams. Fill in your targets for each day. Be realistic when setting the targets, and try your best to stick to them. If you miss a revision period, remember to re-schedule it for another time.
- Check what will be examined and in what ways: identify the topics on your syllabus. Get to know the format of the papers – time, number of questions, types of questions.
- *Make a summary* of the key definitions, theories, empirical evidence, case study examples and diagrams relevant for each topic you are revising.
- Read again the chapters in this book for each topic you are revising. Make sure you have worked through all the questions and activities and can tick the 'confident' box for each element in the revision checklist at the end of each chapter.
- Work out the 'minutes per mark' available for each question in your exam. For example, if you have a 2-hour exam, then you can allocate 1.2 minutes for each mark; so you should allocate 12 minutes for a 10-mark question, 24 minutes for a 20-mark question and so on.

How to tackle your examination

What you do in the exam room depends, in part, on the type of question you are answering.

Essay questions

- Read every question on the examination paper carefully before deciding which questions to answer.
- Answer your 'best' question first, to help gain confidence.
- Make a brief plan for your answer before you begin to write.
- Structure your answer, with an introduction, main body, and conclusion (see earlier) and check that you are answering the question actually set – not the one you wish had been set.
- Throughout your answer bring in relevant economic theory, refer to relevant empirical evidence, draw, label and use relevant diagrams.
- Manage your time effectively. Try not to go over the time allocation for each question. If you have not finished in that time, write a few extra sentences to conclude and leave space to return to the question if you have time later.

Data response questions

There are different types of stimulus-based or data response questions, but all require the same basic approach. Much of what has been written earlier with respect to essay questions also applies here, though you must remember that the purpose of providing data is to test your understanding of the principles contained in the data.

- Base your answer on the data (numerical or textual) you are provided with. Failure to do this will seriously reduce the mark you are awarded.
- Use economic principles to illustrate your points. Search hard for them. They are not always apparent, especially in real-world data.
- Look for trends and relationships in numerical and statistical data. Manipulate any 'raw' or untreated numerical or statistical data to give it meaning, e.g. find measures of central location or dispersion, trend line etc.
- Try to recognise the limitations of any statistical data you are given and to recognise the assumptions on which any conclusions of some extract you are given are based.

Multiple choice questions

- Work out the minutes per question; e.g. 50 multiple choice questions in a one and a half hour exam is 1.8 minutes per question.
- Check there is no penalty for wrong answers. If there is no penalty, make sure you attempt all questions.
- Don't spend too much time on any one question – leave it and return later. The following questions may be easier.
- Towards the end of the exam, if you still have some remaining questions unanswered, have an intelligent guess rather than miss them out.

Final revision checklist

- ❏ Have you revised everything in the 'Revision Checklist' at the start of each chapter and topic?
- ❏ Have you read and made notes on the additional materials in the 'Read to impress' section at the end of each chapter and topic?
- ❏ Can you see how to structure your answer after working through the 'Answer guidelines' for the question at the end of each chapter and topic?
- ❏ Have you tried all the questions and activities for each topic in this book and on the companion website?

Notes

And finally, before the assessment...

Notes

Glossary

Accelerationist theory The theory that unemployment can only be kept below the equilibrium rate at the cost of accelerating inflation.

Accelerator theory A theory to explain the volatility of investment that assumes that the level of investment is dependent on the rate of growth in national income.

Adaptive expectations Backward-looking expectations of a variable based on previous values.

Advances Longer-term credit facilities for households and businesses, including long-term loans like residential mortgages.

Aggregate demand The total level of spending on goods and services made in the economy.

Aggregate supply The total volume of domestically produced goods and services.

Annual rate of inflation The *percentage increase* in the level of prices over a 12-month period.

Appreciation A rise in the free-market exchange rate of the domestic currency against foreign currencies.

Automatic stabilisers Changes in the level of government spending and in payments of tax resulting from changes in national income that help to stabilise the economy.

Autonomous consumption The level of consumption that does not depend on income.

Balance of payments A record of all of a country's transactions with the rest of the world.

Balance of trade (in goods and services) The balance between a country's exports and imports in goods and services.

Bilateral exchange rate The rate at which two currencies can be exchanged.

Bills of exchange Short-term debt instruments sold at discount but redeemed by the issuer at face value.

Broad money The notes and coins held by the non-bank private sector along with its holdings of financial instruments with a maturity of up to five years.

Business cycle The fluctuations in real GDP that result from variations in short-term rates of economic growth.

Capital account A record of the transfer of ownership of non-produced, non-financial assets and of capital transfers.

Capital adequacy The ratio of a bank's capital to its total assets, where the assets are weighted by their level of risk.

Capital deepening An increase in the amount of capital per worker.

Carry trade Investors borrowing funds from countries with lower interest rates and investing them in countries with higher interest rates.

Certificates of deposit A form of time deposit where the depositor is issued with a tradable certificate.

Chain linking The process of applying estimates of the percentage change in the volume of output between consecutive years to the nominal GDP series starting from a chosen base year.

Claimant count An administrative measure of unemployment based on those entitled to the 'Jobseeker's Allowance'.

Consumption smoothing The attempt by households to reduce the variability of their spending despite facing volatile incomes.

Cost-push inflation Inflation arising from persistent increases in the costs of production.

Credit creation The process by which banks increase the money supply through the provision of credit.

Credit cycle The expansion or contraction of credit provided by financial institutions across the business cycle.

Cumulative causation The name given to a chain of events that follows from an event, such as a change in government expenditure or taxation.

Current account The balance of trade in goods and services, plus net income flows and current transfers of money.

Demand-deficient unemployment Unemployment that results from a fall in aggregate demand without a corresponding fall in the real wage rate.

Demand-pull inflation Inflation caused by persistent increases in aggregate demand.

Depreciation A fall in the free-market exchange rate of the domestic currency against foreign currencies.

Diminishing marginal returns The decline in the additional amount of output that results from increasing an input while the quantity of other inputs remains constant.

Discount Window Facility A means by which banks and building societies can borrow gilts (government bonds) from the Bank of England for 30 or 364 days against a wide range of collateral.

Discretionary fiscal policy Deliberate changes in the level of government spending and/or rates of taxation.

Disequilibrium unemployment Unemployment that results from real wages being above the equilibrium level.

Disposable income Household income after the deduction of taxes and the addition of benefits.

Double-dip recession An economy experiencing recession only shortly after exiting a recession.

Dutch disease The name given to the appreciation of a currency following the discovery of new natural resources, which adversely impacts on existing export markets.

Effective exchange rate A trade-weighted average exchange rate allowing us to compare a country's currency with a bundle of other currencies.

Equilibrium level of national income The level of national income matched by an equivalent expenditure on domestically produced goods and services. It is also the level of national income at which the sum of injections into the inner flow is matched by the sum of withdrawals from the inner flow.

Equilibrium unemployment The difference between those willing to take employment at current wage rates and those actually able to.

Expectations-augmented Phillips curve A short-run Phillips curve whose vertical position depends on the expected rate of inflation.

External balance The name given to the situation when the current account of the balance of payments is in balance.

Factor incomes Incomes that result from the services provided by the factors of production.

Final goods and services Goods and services when purchased by their final or ultimate user rather than as components of a good or service.

Financial account A record of cross-border transactions involving financial instruments, such as deposits with financial institutions.

Financial instruments Financial products resulting in one party having a financial claim over another.

Financial intermediaries Financial institutions that bring together those economic agents looking to borrow and those looking to save.

Fiscal policy Changes in the level of government spending and/or rates of taxation.

Fixed exchange rate regime Where the authorities intervene in an attempt to 'fix' the exchange rate at a specific level.

Floating exchange rate Where exchange rates are determined by demand and supply without government intervention in the foreign exchange market.

Forward exchange rates Exchange rates agreed today at which currencies will be exchanged at some future point of time.

Frictional (search) unemployment Frictions in the labour market, such as imperfect information, which cause unemployment as workers search for employment and firms search for employees.

Game theory An analysis of strategic interactions among economic agents, such as those between workers, firms and policy-makers.

GDP deflator The name given to the average price level of domestically produced goods and services.

GDP per capita GDP per head of the population.

Gearing (or leverage) The ratio of debt capital to share capital.

General government The collective name for local and central government.

Gross domestic product (GDP) The market value of domestically produced goods and services.

Gross national income The income earned by domestic residents from economic activity regardless of where that activity occurred. It is estimated by adding net income from abroad to GDP.

Human capital The skills, expertise and health of the population.

Induced investment Investment by firms in response to increased demand for their goods and services.

Inflation bias Excessive inflation resulting from workers and other suppliers of inputs maintaining high inflation rate expectations.

Inflation A rise in the *level* of prices.

Injections Spending on firms' goods and services by purchasers other than domestic households.

Interest rate parity The theory that international differences in interest rates should reflect expected movements in currencies.

Intermediate goods and services Goods and services used as inputs that become components of the final good or service.

Internal balance The name given to the situation when an economy's aggregate demand equals its potential output.

International business cycle Fluctuations in global output that are frequently mirrored by national economies.

Labour force People who are economically active and either in employment or unemployed.

Law of comparative advantage The potential for two countries to gain from trade because of differences in their opportunity costs of producing various goods.

Liquidity ratio The proportion of a financial institution's total assets held in liquid form, that is liquid assets/total assets.

Liquidity The ease with which a financial product can be turned into a sum of cash of known value.

Long-run equilibrium real exchange rate The real exchange rate at which an economy achieves both internal and external balance.

Long-term economic growth The change in real GDP over an extended period of time, perhaps over several generations.

Managed float (dirty float) A system of floating exchange rates where the authorities occasionally intervene to affect exchange rates.

Macroeconomic equilibrium. The equilibrium that occurs when the total demand for domestically produced goods and services equals the total output of domestically produced goods and services.

Marginal propensity to consume (*mpc*) The proportion of an increase in national income spent by households.

Marginal propensity to consume domestically produced goods and services (*mpc_d*) The proportion of an increase in national income spent on domestically produced goods and services.

Marginal propensity to import (*mpm*) The proportion of an increase in national income spent on imports.

Marginal propensity to save (*mps*) The proportion of an increase in national income saved by households.

Marginal propensity to tax (*mpt*) The proportion of an increase in national income taken in tax (net of benefits).

Marginal propensity to withdrawal (*mpw*) The proportion of an increase in national income that flows outside of the inner flow between households and firms.

Market loans Short-term loans from other banks and financial institutions.

Maturity transformation The process by which financial institutions borrow short from depositors and lend long to borrowers.

Medium of exchange The characteristic of money as an acceptable means of payment in economic transactions.

Monetary financial institutions The name given to deposit-taking institutions, including banks, building societies and the central bank.

Monetary policy Actions taken by the authorities to affect the quantity or price of money.

Money multiplier The number of times greater is the change in broad money following a change in narrow money.

Narrow money Notes and coins in circulation outside the Bank of England.

Net national income The income earned by domestic residents after taking into account the depreciation of the nation's physical resources from economic activity.

Nominal GDP Another name for actual GDP where estimates are affected both by the volume of output and by the prices of the output.

Open-market operations (OMOs) The sale or purchase by the central bank of government debt instruments in the open market.

Operational standing facilities Central bank facilities by which individual banks can deposit reserves or borrow reserves.

Other financial corporations Non-deposit-taking financial institutions, such as insurance companies and pension funds, typically used for longer-term investments.

Phillips curve A curve showing the relationship between price inflation and unemployment. The original Phillips curve captured the empirical relationship between wage inflation and unemployment in the UK between 1861 and 1957.

Physical capital (non-financial fixed assets) Inputs that can be used for a protracted period of time, usually more than one year, in the production of goods and services.

Political business cycle The idea that governments deliberately attempt to affect the economy, including the path of real GDP, to increase the likelihood of their re-election.

Potential output The economy's output level when resources are being employed at normal levels of utilisation and which is sustainable over the longer term.

Precautionary demand for money The motivation to hold money due to uncertainty and unforeseen circumstances.

Production function A function that describes the relationship between inputs and output. A production function can be for either an individual firm or an economy as a whole.

Productivity shock A shock that affects the effectiveness of those inputs used in production.

Propagating mechanisms The name given by real business cycle theorists to the means by which shocks to the economy can have enduring effects.

Public-sector net borrowing (PSNB) The difference between the expenditures of the public sector and its receipts from taxation and other revenues from public corporations.

Purchasing-power parity exchange rate The exchange rate that allows a given amount of money in one country to buy the same amount of goods in another country using the currency of the other country.

Purchasing-power parity The idea that the nominal exchange rate adjusts to offset differences in countries' inflation rates.

Quantitative easing Large-scale open-market operations to increase the supply of money.

Rational expectations Expectations based on all available and relevant information such that economic agents' errors are random.

Real balance effect The impact on the purchasing power of our financial assets resulting from changes in the average price level of domestically produced goods and services.

Real business cycles Business cycles caused by shocks to aggregate supply that persist, thereby affecting potential output.

Real exchange rate The actual exchange rate adjusted by the average price of a country's exports relative to the average price of its imports.

Real GDP A constant-price estimate of the value of the economy's output measured at the prices of a chosen base year.

Real wage unemployment Unemployment that occurs because the current real wage rate is above the equilibrium real wage rate, causing an excess supply of labour.

Recession Declining output (real GDP) for two or more consecutive quarters.

Replacement investment Investment by firms to replace capital because of wear and tear or it becoming obsolete.

Reserve averaging The process whereby individual banks manage their average level of overnight reserves between MPC meetings using the Bank of England's operational standing facilities and/or the interbank market.

Reserve balances Accounts held by commercial banks at the Bank of England that act as a form of current account for banks and that allow the settlement of payments between banks.

Reverse repos The assets, such as government bonds, purchased as part of a repo operation.

Risk transformation The 'spreading of risk' by financial institutions by lending to a large number of customers.

Sale and repurchase agreements (repos) Secured loans where the borrower sells assets, such as government bonds, in exchange for the deposit of cash and agrees to buy the assets back at a fixed price on a fixed date.

Securitisation Where assets backed by regular cash flows are turned into tradable securities.

Share capital A long-term source of finance obtained by issuing shares that gives ownership rights to the holders.

Short-term economic growth The change in real GDP over short periods of time. Commonly short-term economic growth is measured over 3 months or 12 months.

Sight deposits Deposits that can be withdrawn on demand without penalty.

Speculative demand for money The motivation to hold money because of the current or expected return on alternative forms of holding wealth.

Standardised unemployment rate The percentage of the workforce of working age without work who are available for work and are actively seeking employment.

Store of wealth The ability of economic agents to hold their wealth as money and be able to purchase goods and services in the future.

Structural (mismatch) unemployment Unemployment that results from a mismatch between the skills of potential workers and those demanded by employers or from a mismatch between the location of potential workers and employers.

Substitution effects The incentive to switch to (or from) domestically produced goods and services when the average price level of domestically produced goods and services falls (or rises).

Supply-side shock A shock that affects the position of the aggregate supply curve by affecting the amount that firms are collectively willing to supply at different price levels.

Surprise inflation The situation where additional inflation, perhaps generated by policy-makers, causes the actual rate of inflation to be greater than expected.

The multiplier The number of times greater the change in national income is compared with the initial change in aggregate demand that caused it.

Time deposits Deposits where notice of withdrawal is needed or where a penalty is incurred for withdrawal.

Time lags Lags in the implementation and impact of fiscal policy that might result in greater fluctuations of real GDP than would otherwise be the case.

Transactions demand for money The motivation to hold wealth as money in order to engage in transactions.

Transmission mechanism The means by which policy changes affect policy targets, such as an inflation rate target.

Withdrawals (or leakages) Incomes of domestic households or firms that leak out of the inner flow between households and firms.

Notes

Index

Entries in bold are also listed in the Glossary on pages 209-216

accelerationist theory (inflation) 157–9
definition 159
as game theory 159–60
accelerator theory of investment 90
definition 91
AD-AS model
changes in aggregate demand and macroeconomic equilibrium 71–2
changes in aggregate supply and macroeconiomic equilibrium 73–4
macroeconomic equilibrium 70–4
short-run aggregate supply 59–66, 73–4
adaptive expectations 160
definition 160
advances 115
aggregate demand 14
accelerationist theory 157–9
changes in and impact on national income 44–50, 71–2
changes in and macroeconomic equilibrium 71–2
and circular flow of income 32–4
and consumption 38–9, 88–9
definition 14, 32, 66, 68
and exports 36, 42
fluctuations *see separate entry*
government purchases 42
and imports 36, 42
income-expenditure approach (Keynesian cross-presentation) 48–50
increase in - factors causing 69
increase in - longer-term impact 72
increase in - short-term impact 71–2
and inflation 149
and interest rates 23
internal balance 188–9
and investment 42, 95
and net savings 39
nominal compared with real 98
and shifts in ADC 68–9
and taxation 39–40
withdrawals-injections presentation of Keynesian model 46–8
see also AD-AS model; Keynesian model, and components of aggregate demand - assumptions
aggregate demand curve 66–9
description 66–7, 68
shifts - effects on business cycle/GDP 86–8
shifts and variables 68–9
substitution effects 67
aggregate demand, fluctuations 86–98
expectations 96–8
financial system 94–6
fiscal policy 92–4
household consumption 88–90
impact on GDP 86
investment 90–2
wage contracts 96–8
aggregate supply
definition 59
fluctuations *see separate entry*
and inflation 150
and investment 95
short-run, changes in 73–4
see also AD-AS model

aggregate supply curve
  description 59
  shifts in 98–100
aggregate supply curve, short-run 59–66
  inputs and costs 60–1
  production function 60
  slope 60, 61
  stylised (hypothetical) 61–2
  variables that shift 64–6
aggregate supply, fluctuations 98–101
  real business cycle theory 100–1
  shifts of AS curve 98–100
annual rate of inflation 12, 148
  definition 13, 148
appreciation (exchange rate) 184–5
  definition 185
automatic stabilisers 92–3
  definition 93
autonomous consumption 39

balance of payments 17–19, 170, 174–8
  capital account 17, 175, 176
  credit items 174
  current account 17, 174–5, 190, 191
  debit items 174
  definition 174
  and exchange rates 176
  external balance 190–1
  financial account 17, 175, 176
  net errors and omission item 176
  UK 2011 177
  UK as percentage of GDP 178
balance of trade 17–18
Bank of England 108
  aggregate amount of reserves and
    credit creation 125
  bank note issue 238
  bank rate 14, 22–3, 112, 127
  as banker to government 128
  banks' reserve balances 110, 111,
    114, 128, 129–31
  cash ratio deposits 115
  Consolidated Fund 128
  Discount Window Facility 132
  Exchange Equalisation Account 175
  Financial Conduct Authority 128
  Financial Policy Committee 128
  financial stability 128
  inflation control 14, 22, 161

  interest rates 22, 112, 127, 128,
    161–3
  monetary policy 127, 128–32
  Monetary Policy Committee 14, 112,
    114, 127, 128
  open-market operations 130
  operational standing facilities 130,
    131
  Prudential Regulation Authority 128
  quantitative easing 121, 125, 132
  reserve averaging 130, 131, 132
  reserves, flows to and from 175
  role 127–8
banks
  balance sheets see separate entry
  balances at Bank of England 114–15
  capital adequacy 119, 120
  cash ratio deposits 115
  Discount Window Facility 132
  gearing (leverage) 118
  interbank rates 130
  liquidity ratio 118, 124–5
  long-term credit 95
  reserve balances at Bank of England
    110, 111, 114, 128, 129–31
  short-term credit 95, 115
  see also financial institutions;
    financial system; monetary
    financial institutions
banks' balance sheets 95, 113–20
  aggregate 116–17, 124
  assets 114–15
  liabilities 113–14
  share capital 114
Basel Committee 119
benefits, and circular flow of income
    model 35
bilateral exchange rate 178–9
  definition 180
bills of exchange 115
bonds 115
broad money 122–3, 124, 125–6
  definition 122
building societies see financial
    institutions; monetary financial
    institutions
business cycle 7, 82–6
  characteristics 82–3
  definition 8, 82

impact of fluctuations in aggregate demand 86–8

impact of fluctuations in aggregate supply 98–101

impact of government 20, 92–4

international 85–6, 172

phases 83

real 100–1

capital

changes in and shifts in SRAS curve 65

physical *see* **physical capital**

capital account (balance of payments) 17, 175

definition 176

capital adequacy 119

definition 120

capital deepening 65, 100

definition 101

carry trade 193

definition 193

central banks

independence and inflation bias 162–3

independence and Phillips curve 161–3

monetary policy 22, 127

see also Bank of England

certificates of deposit 113, 114

chain linking 6–7

definition 7

circular flow of income model 30, 31–7

and aggregate demand 32–4, 51

equilibrium 37

exports 36

factor incomes 32

financial institutions 34

and general government 35–7

government benefits 35

imports 35–6

injections and withdrawals 32–4

and investment 33–4

net taxation 35

public and foreign sectors 35–7

and savings 34

claimant count 15, 142, 143

collateralised debt obligations (CDOs) 117, 118

comparative advantage, law of 173

Consolidated Fund 128

Consumer Price Index (CPI) inflation rate 13–14, 128, 148

consumer spending *see* consumption

consumption

autonomous 39

and availability of credit 41

as component of aggregate demand 38–9, 88–9

determinants 40–1

and financial institutions 40–1

impact of fluctuations in aggregate demand 88–90

marginal propensity to consume 38, 39, 88

smoothing 88–90

consumption smoothing 88–90

definition 89

cost-push inflation 150

definition 150

credit

availability and consumption 41, 90, 92

long-term 95, 111

short-term 95, 115

credit creation 123–6

and aggregate amount of reserves 125

definition 124

and demand for money 125

liquidity ratio 124–5

money multiplier 125–6

credit cycle 95

cross-border transactions in goods and services 17–19

and exchange rates 19

cumulative causation 45

current account (balance of payments) 17, 174–5, 190, 191

definition 17, 176

trade in goods and services 17–19

demand-deficient unemployment 146–7

definition 147

demand-pull inflation 149–50

definition 149

deposits 113–14

certificates of 113, 114

sight 113, 114

time 113, 114

depreciation (exchange rate) 184
    definition 185
diminishing marginal returns 61
Discount Window Facility 132
discretionary fiscal policy 21, 93–4
    definition 94
disequilibrium unemployment 16, 143–5
    definition 143
    demand-deficient 146–7
    real wage 146, 147
    types 146–7
disposable income 39
    and consumer spending 40–1
    definition 40
double-dip recession 83
Dutch disease 191–2
    definition 192

economic crisis late 2000s 94–5, 96, 112
    and UK monetary policy 131–2
economic growth 80
    annual rates in UK 1950-2010 7
    and exchange rates 185
    international comoparison 86
    and investment 90–2
    meaning of 7
    and real GDP 7
    and shifts in SRAS curve 65–6
    short-term 7
    short-term compared with long-term
        80
    UK 1956-2011 81
    see also **business cycle; recession**
economic interdependence 170
effective exchange rate 178–9
    definition 180
equilibrium level of national income
    definition 37
    income-expenditure approach
        (Keynesian cross-presentation)
        48–50
    withdrawals-injections presentation
        of Keynesian model 46–8
equilibrium unemployment 16, 143–6
    definition 143
    frictional 145, 146
    seasonal 146
    structural 145–6
    types of 145–6

Exchange Equalisation Account 175
exchange rates 170, 178–83
    appreciation 184–5
    bilateral 178–9, 180
    cross-border transactions in goods
        and services 19
    depreciation 184, 185
    and economic growth 185
    effective 178–9, 180
    fixed regime 182–4, 195–6
    floating 178–9, 194–6
    fluctuations *see separate entry*
    forward 195
    and inflation 183–4, 185, 189–92
    instability 194–5
    and interest rates 183–4, 185, 192
    intervention 182–4
    long-run equilbrium real 191
    long-run real 190–2
    managed (dirty) float 182
    nominal 187–8, 189–90
    purchasing-power parity rate 9–10
    real 184–5, 187–8, 191
    speculation 185, 192–3, 194
exchange rates, fluctuations 184–94
    carry trade 193
    depreciation of UK£ from 2007 187–9
    and inflation 185, 189–92
    interest rate parity 192
    interest rates 192
    long-run real exchange rate 190–2
    movements in currency demand and
        supply 184–5
    purchasing-power parity 189–90
    and speculation 192–3
expectations
    accelerationist theory 157–9
    adaptive 160
    and aggregate demand 69, 96–8
    and economic activity 96
    and inflation 151, 155–63, 162
    and prices 96
    rational 160
expectations-augmented Phillips curve
    155–63
    definition 156
exports
    and aggregate demand 36, 42
    and circular flow of income model 36

external balance 190–1
  definition 191

factor incomes 32
final goods and services 3
  definition 4
financial account (balance of payments)
  17, 175
  definition 176
financial crisis late 2000s 94–5, 96, 112
  and UK monetary policy 131–2
financial derivatives 175
financial institutions
  and circular flow of income model 34
  global interdependence 171–2
  and household consumption 40–1
  monetary *see* **monetary financial
    institutions**
  other than monetary 109
  role 108
  types 109–10
financial instruments 113–20
  definition 113
financial intermediaries 109
  definition 110
financial markets, global interdependence
  171–2
financial stability 128
financial system
  credit cycle 95
  and fluctuations in aggregate
    demand 94–6
  long-term credit 95
  short-term credit 95
  see also banks
fiscal policy 20–2, 23
  automatic stabilisers 92–3
  contractionary 20–1
  definition 21
  discretionary 21, 93–4
  expansionary 20
  and fluctuations in aggregate
    demand 92–4
  time lags 94
fixed exchange rate regime 182–4
  advantages and disadvantages
    195–6
  definition 182
floating exchange rate

  advantages and disadvantages
    194–6
  definition 180
  determination 178–9
foreign exchange market 170
forward exchange rates 195
  definition 195
frictional (search) unemployment 145,
  146

game theory 159–60
  definition 160
GDP *see* **gross domestic product**
GDP deflator 5, 13, 66, 148
  definition 6, 59
  impact of increase in aggregate
    demand 71–2
  and shifts in ADC 68
  and short-run aggregate supply 73–4
GDP per capita 9–10
  definition 10
gearing (leverage) 118
gilts 22, 115
global interdependencies 171–3
  international business cycle 172
  through finance 171–2
  through trade 171, 173
globalisation 85
goods and services
  final 3, 4
  intermediate 3, 4
  marginal propensity to consume
    domestically produced 43
government, impact on business cycle
  92–4
government benefits
  and aggregate demand 69
  and circular flow of income model 35
government, general
  and circular flow of income model
    35–7
  definition 35
government intervention 19–23
  allocative effects 20
  and business cycle 20
  distributive effects 20
  fiscal policy 20–2, 23
  monetary policy 22–3
  short and long-term impact 20

government purchases, and aggregate
demand 42
government spending, and aggregate
demand 69
gross domestic product 3–11
comparison over time 5–8
comparison of various countries 8–12
definition 4
description 3
excluded economic activities 3–4
impact of fluctuations in aggregate
demand 86–7
nominal 5–6
per capita 9–10
real 6
see also **business cycle; recession**
gross national income 4
definition 5

household consumption *see* consumption
housing market 111
human capital
definition 65
and shifts in SRAS curve 65
Human Development Index 11–12

imports
and aggregate demand 36, 42
circular flow of income model 35–6
marginal propensity to import 42
income
disposable 39, 40
see also circular flow of income model
induced investment 90
definition 91
inflation 22, 148–51
accelerationist theory 157–9
and aggregate demand 149
and aggregate supply 150
annual rate 12, 13, 140, 148
bias 162–3
causes 149–51
Consumer Price Index (CPI) 13–14, 148
control of 128–32
cost-push 150
costs of 148–9
CPI rate 128
definition 13, 148
demand-pull 149–50

and exchange rates 183–4, 185,
189–92
expectations 151, 155–63, 162
measurement of 12–14
menu costs 148
pay negotiations 96, 97
redistribution costs 148–9
surprise 160, 161
uncertainty costs 149
and unemployment, *see also* Phillips
curve
and unemployment in UK 140–1,
154–5
inflation bias 162–3
definition 162
injections
circular flow of income 32–4
definition 33
inputs, and output - production function 60
interbank rates 130
interbank 130
interest rate parity 192
definition 192
interest rates
and aggregate demand 23, 69, 128–9
Bank of England 22, 127, 128
effect of 128–9
and exchange rates 183–4, 185, 192
impact on inflation 128–9
substitution effect 67
intermediate goods and services 3
definition 4
internal balance 188–9
definition 191
international business cycles 85–6, 172
definition 86
investment
accelerator theory 90, 91
and aggregate demand 42, 90–2, 95
and aggregate supply 95
and circular flow of income 33–4
and economic growth 90–2
induced 90, 91
replacement 90–1

Keynesian model 30, 38–51
and aggregate demand *see* Keynesian
model, and components of
aggregate demand - assumptions

changes in aggregate demand and
impact on national income 44–5
equilibrium level of national income
- income-expenditure approach
(Keynesian cross-presentation)
48–50
equilibrium level of national income -
withdrawals-injections presentation
46–8
limitations 51
marginal propensity to withdrawal
43–4
Keynesian model, and components of
aggregate demand - assumptions
38–43
consumption 38–9
exports 42
government purchases 42
imports 42
investment 42
savings, net 39
summary 46
taxes, net 39–40

labour force 142, 143
law of comparative advantage 173
liquidity 110–11
definition 111
liquidity ratio 118, 124–5
loans (banks) 111, 112
see also credit
long-run real exchange rate 190–2
definition 191
long-term economic growth 8
definition 8
see also economic growth

macroeconomic equilibrium
in AD-AS model 70–4
changes in aggregate demand 71–2
changes in aggregate supply 73–4
definition 70
macroeconomics
compared with microeconomics 2
description 2
managed (dirty) float 182
definition 182
marginal propensity to consume 38, 88
definition 39, 89

marginal propensity to consume
domestically produced goods and
services 43
definition 44
marginal propensity to import 42
marginal propensity to save 39
marginal propensity to tax 40
marginal propensity to withdrawal 43–4,
45
definition 44
marginal returns, diminishing 61
market loans 115
maturity transformation 112
measurement of economic activity
gross domestic product see separate
entry
gross national income 4, 5
net national income 4, 5
medium of exchange 120
microeconomics
compared with macroeconomics 2
description 2
monetary financial institutions 109
balance sheets see banks' balance
sheets
balances at Bank of England 110,
111, 114–15, 128, 129–31
definition 110
deposit accounts 110, 111, 112
deposits 113–14
financial instruments 113–20
functions 110–12
inter-bank lending 112
investments 115
loans 111, 112
long-term lending 111
maturity transformation 112
securitisation 117–19
short-term lending 115
as source of liquidity 110–11
monetary policy 22–3, 127, 128–32
definition 22
and financial crisis 131–2
money
demand for 125, 126–7
functions 120–1
as medium of exchange 120
precautionary demand 126, 127
speculative demand 126, 127

money (*cont.*)
    as store of wealth 120, 121
    supply *see separate entry*
    tansactions demand 126, 127
money multiplier 125–6
    definition 126
money supply
    and aggregate demand 69
    broad money 122–3, 124
    credit creation 123–6
    measures 121–3
    money multiplier 125–6
    narrow money 121, 122
    quantitative easing 121, 132
    relationship between broad and
        narrow money 125–6
mortgage markets 111
multiplier 45

narrow money 121, 125–6
    definition 122
national income
    equilibrium level 37
    equilibrium level - income-expenditure
        approach (Keynesian cross-
        presentation) 48–50
    equilibrium level - withdrawals-
        injections presentation of
        Keynesian model 46–8
    impact of changes in aggregate
        demand 44–50, 71–2
national well-being 4–5
net national income 4
    definition 5
nominal GDP 5–6
    compared with real GDP 6–7
    definition 6
    description 5

open-market operations 130
operational standing facilities 130, 131
opportunity costs in production 173
other financial institutions 109
    definition 110
output
    impact of increase in aggregate
        demand 71, 72
    and inputs - production function 60
    potential 61–2

potential - estimation 62–3
    potential compared with actual 62–3
    and price changes 64
    and short-run aggregate supply 73–4
output gaps 62–3

Phillips curve 141, 151–63
    accelerationist theory 157–9
    basic graph 152
    and central bank independence 161–3
    definition 151
    expectations-augmented 155–63
    inflation expectations 155–63
    inflation and unemployment
        relationship in UK 154–5
    mechanism 153–4
    rational expectations and wage-
        setting 159–61
physical capital 60–1
    definition 60
political business cycle 93
    definition 94
potential output 61–2
    definition 61
    estimation 62–3
precautionary demand for money 126, 127
prices
    changes in and output volume 64
    changes in and SRAS curve 64
    and expectations 96
    impact of increase in aggregate
        demand 72
    macroeconomic equilibrium 70
    and short-run aggregate supply 73–4
production, opportunity costs 173
production function 60
productivity shocks 99–100
    definition 100
propagating mechanisms 100
    definition 101
public sector, and circular flow of income
    model 35
public-sector net borrowing (PSNB) 21–2
    definition 21
purchasing-power parity 189–90
    definition 190
purchasing-power parity exchange rate
    9–10
    definition 10

quantitative easing 121, 125, 132
  definition 132

rational expectations 160
  definition 160
real balance effect 67, 68
real business cycles 100–1
  definition 100
real exchange rate 184–5, 187–8,
  191
  definition 187
real GDP 6
  chain linking 6–7
  compared wth nominal GDP 6–7
  definition 6
  and economic growth 7
real wage unemployment 146
  definition 147
recession 83
  definition 83
  double-dip 83
  UK since 1955 - depth and duration
  84–5
replacement investment 90–1
  definition 91
reserve averaging 130, 131, 132
reserve balances 110, 111, 114, 128,
  129–31
  open-market operations 130
  operational standing facilities 130,
  131
  reserve averaging 130, 131, 132
reserves, flows to and from, and balance
  of payments 175
reverse repos 115
risk transformation 110, 111

sale and repurchase agreements (repos)
  113, 114
savings 113, 114
  and aggregate demand 39
  and circular flow of income 34
  marginal propensity to save 39
  net 39
seasonal unemployment 146
second-hand goods 3
securitisation 117–19
services see goods and services
share capital 114

short-term economic growth 7
  definition 8
  see also economic growth
speculation, and exchange rates 192–3,
  194
speculative demand for money 126, 127
standardised unemployment rate 15,
  142, 143
storing wealth 120, 121
structural (mismatch) unemployment
  145–6
substitution effects
  aggregate demand curve 67
  definition 68
supply-side shocks 99
  definition 100
surprise inflation 160
  definition 161

taxation
  and aggregate demand 39–40, 69
  and circular flow of income model
  35
  fiscal policy 20–2
  marginal propensity to tax 40
technological progress, and shifts in SRAS
  curve 65
time deposits 113, 114
time lags 94
trade
  global interdependence 171, 173
  see also trade, international
trade, international
  law of comparative advantage
  173
  reasons for 173
transactions demand for money
  126, 127
transmission mechanism 128
Treasury bills 22

underground markets 4
unemployment 142–8
  disequilibrium 16, 143–5
  equilibrium 16, 143–6
  flows 142
  and inflation 140–1, 154–5
    see also Phillips curve
  rate - definition 140

unemployment - measurement of 15–16,
  142–3
    claimant count 15, 142, 143
    standardised rate 15, 142, 143

wage contracts, and fluctuations in
  aggregate demand 96–8

wages, inflation and unemployment *see*
  Phillips curve
withdrawal, marginal propensity to
  44
withdrawals (or leakages)
  circular flow of income 32–4
  definition 33